c/o DearJohn.

me

cato

arak—

Devon Steam

MICHAEL WELCH

Capital Transport

ISBN 978-1-85414-374-7

Published by
Capital Transport Publishing Ltd
www.capitaltransport.com

Printed by Parksons Graphics

Front Cover: Judging by the amount of steam leaking at the front end, 'Modified Hall' Class 4-6-0 No.6965 *Thirlestaine Hall* was overdue for a 'valves and pistons' examination when this picture was taken on 14th July 1958. The locomotive is, however, nicely turned out with both its copper capped chimney and safety valve bonnet polished to perfection. Note the lower quadrant signal which is located on the opposite side of the line to which it refers, doubtless to improve sighting for the enginemen. The amount of cloud in the sky suggests that the photographer was very fortunate to have the sun shining as the train passed his vantage point. *R.C. Riley*

Title page: County of Devon in Devon! Few photographs of 'County' Class locomotives were submitted for use in this album, so the author was especially pleased to see this portrait of No.1005 *County of Devon* which was taken at Laira shed on 25th September 1960. Judging by its gleaming paintwork No.1005 had recently benefitted from a visit to Swindon works. A fine sight indeed. *R.C. Riley*

Back Cover: An O2 Class 0-4-4T crosses Calstock viaduct with a Plymouth to Callington train just as a small motor boat passes underneath. Luck was obviously on the photographer's side! The graceful 12-arch viaduct has 60ft spans and opened in 1908. This shot probably dates from the early 1950s. *Colin Hogg*

Introduction

When asked to nominate their favourite English counties most people would probably include Devon and for many it would be top of their list. The very mention of names such as Torquay, llfracombe and Exmouth conjure up picture-postcard scenes of the sun shining from a clear blue sky upon happy holiday-makers strolling along the promenade or basking on the beach. Those seeking peace and tranquillity, however, could seek refuge in the beautiful countryside that offers lush, secluded river valleys or, in complete contrast, on the vast expanses of Dartmoor which has some of the most challenging and wild terrain in Great Britain.

The growth of the railway system enabled the delights of Devon to be enjoyed by people from all corners of Great Britain and, perhaps, the most significant developments were the opening of the route from London to Exeter via Bristol in 1844 and its extension on to Plymouth which opened for business in 1849. The line from Waterloo via Salisbury reached Exeter Queen Street station (later Central) in 1860 and this line also eventually reached Plymouth via Okehampton. These comprised the main trunk lines serving the county, but there was also a comprehensive network of branch lines and it is probably fair to say that virtually every centre of population of any consequence was rail-served. While the first branch to be opened was that from Tiverton Junction to Tiverton in June 1848 this was not outstanding scenically and, perhaps, the best line in this respect was the spectacular byway across the wilds of Dartmoor from Yelverton to Princetown which climbed to a height of 1,350 feet above sea level with a ruling gradient of 1 in 40. Another noteworthy route was the section between Mortehoe and llfracombe where the precipitous nature of the drop down from the summit to llfracombe – two miles at 1 in 36 – must have been quite an experience for passengers. Far less intimidating was a leisurely trip along the Hemyock branch from Tiverton Junction alongside the placid waters of the river Culm, an absolute gem of a line if ever there was one. This line was reputed to have the slowest passenger trains anywhere in the country which probably increased its appeal to railway aficionados, if not the local populace. While the construction of the Tiverton branch was an early venture, Devon was also home to the Torrington to Halwill Junction line which was one of the last routes to be built in Great Britain, not being completed until 1925. This was cheaply constructed in part along the trackbed of a former narrow-gauge mineral line and had an atmosphere all of its own, with obscure halts hidden away in woodland and mixed trains timetabled on a regular basis.

The Great Western Railway (GWR) started to promote holiday traffic to Devon as early as 1904, this being done through a series of publications which extolled the pleasure and enjoyment of visiting particular areas and invariably this publicity material was produced in co-operation with a specific resort. In 1906 a booklet about Devon titled 'The Shore of the Sea Kings' was published and this enthusiastically described the county as 'one of the great holiday haunts of the Empire'. Devon's alluring holiday resorts were also promoted through a series of lantern slides, of which a hundred sets were apparently available for showing to clubs, schools and similar groups and, as if this was not enough, the GWR enterprisingly marketed a selection of jigsaw puzzles to promote its services and encourage leisure travel. Perhaps the most important factor in the promotion of services from the London area to Devon was the opening in 1906 of the Castle Cary to Taunton line – dubbed 'the new direct route to the west'– one of the very last stretches of main line railway to be opened in Great Britain which certainly revolutionised travel to the west country. Prior to the opening of this route trains had been forced to go 'the great way round' and the commissioning of this section brought huge benefits, dramatically reduced travelling times and, in effect, brought Devon much nearer to the Capital – or so it seemed. The GWR served the more popular seaside resorts, such as Dawlish, Teignmouth and Torquay, but the Southern Railway was not to be outdone and July 1926 saw the inauguration of the 'Atlantic Coast Express' which, by virtue of its multi-portioned formation and exceptionally fast schedule, became one of the best-known long-distance expresses in the country. The 'ACE', as the train was known colloquially, provided separate through portions from Waterloo to many holiday destinations and in the summer 1957 timetable portions to Sidmouth, Exmouth and llfracombe were advertised besides points across the border in Cornwall. In addition to the famous 'Atlantic Coast Express', on summer Saturdays many other expresses ran from Waterloo to locations on the east Devon coast while llfracombe, the jewel of the north Devon coast, was also a favourite destination despite the much longer journey time.

In many respects the 1950s were the heyday of railways in Devon as the introduction of paid holidays after the Second World War sparked a massive upsurge in week-end holiday travel as the masses converged on the county which was arguably the most popular holiday destination in Great Britain. This was an age before private motoring became commonplace and Londoners comprised, no doubt, one of the largest contingents, but overnight services were run from points in the north of England and the Midlands and, amazingly, on one occasion an observer at Newton Abbot recorded no fewer than 38 loaded westbound passenger trains during an overnight period, though not all were heading for destinations in Devon. On the debit side many hopelessly uneconomic branch lines in the county, with just a handful of trains a day, started to be pruned as BR faced increasing criticism regarding its mounting deficit and many lovely lines featured in this album are now just a distant memory. Perhaps it would be inappropriate to dwell too much on this sad period but many lines were lost and some of the closures seemed particularly savage, allegations being made that some had been motivated by inter-regional rivalry. Certainly the Western Region (WR) appeared determined to eliminate as many former Southern Region (SR) routes as possible and the complete closure of part of the SR Exeter to Plymouth line between Okehampton and Bere Alston, which served the sizeable town of Tavistock, seemed especially harsh. This route would have provided a useful diversionary route to the WR coastal route via Teignmouth which was vulnerable in the event of extreme weather conditions and its closure seemed really short-sighted, particularly as sections at each end of the route remain *in situ* today.

Compilation of this album has given me enormous pleasure but could not have been achieved without assistance from a large number of people, first and foremost the many photographers who had the foresight to record the railway scene before it changed forever. Chris Evans, Dave Fakes, John Langford, Graham Mallinson, Terry Phillips and Ian Pringle have scrutinized the original manuscript and suggested many corrections and improvements which have certainly enhanced the final product. Mike Esau, Tony Hillman and Rodney Lissenden have kindly provided slides and prints from photographic collections in their care while Les Dench supplied the luggage labels. Design and typesetting by Lucy Frontani and Cat Bond.

Michael Welch
Burgess Hill, West Sussex
August 2013

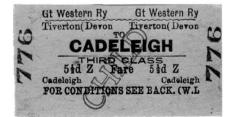

Contents

Axminster to Exeter	6
Lyme Regis Branch	14
Seaton Branch	18
Sidmouth Branch	20
Exmouth Branch	22
Taunton to Exeter	25
Taunton to Barnstaple	31
Hemyock Branch	34
Tiverton to Tiverton Junction	38
Exe Valley Line	40
Exeter to Ilfracombe	44
Exeter to Launceston	50
Exeter to Plymouth via Okehampton	56
Barnstaple to Torrington	66
Torrington to Halwill Junction	68
Exeter to Newton Abbot	73
Newton Abbot to Plymouth	77
Newton Abbot to Kingswear	89
Brixham Branch	91
Teign Valley Line	92
Moretonhampstead Branch	95
Ashburton Branch	98
Kingsbridge Branch	100
Plymouth to Launceston	103
Princetown Branch	109
Turnchapel Branch	111

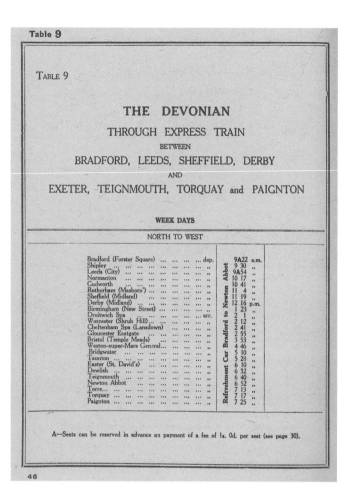

Table 9

TABLE 9

THE DEVONIAN

THROUGH EXPRESS TRAIN

BETWEEN

BRADFORD, LEEDS, SHEFFIELD, DERBY

AND

EXETER, TEIGNMOUTH, TORQUAY and PAIGNTON

WEEK DAYS

NORTH TO WEST

Bradford (Forster Square) ... ... dep.		9A22 a.m.
Shipley ... ... ,,		9 30 ,,
Leeds (City) ... ... ,,		9A54 ,,
Normanton ... ... ,,		10 17 ,,
Cudworth ... ... ,,		10 41 ,,
Rotherham (Masbro') ... ... ,,		11 4 ,,
Sheffield (Midland) ... ... ,,		11 19 ,,
Derby (Midland) ... ... ,,		12 16 p.m.
Birmingham (New Street) ... ... ,,		1 23 ,,
Droitwich Spa ... ... arr.		2 1 ,,
Worcester (Shrub Hill) ... ... ,,		2 12 ,,
Cheltenham Spa (Lansdown) ... ... ,,		2 41 ,,
Gloucester Eastgate ... ... ,,	Refreshment Car Bradford to Newton Abbot	2 55 ,,
Bristol (Temple Meads) ... ... ,,		3 53 ,,
Weston-super-Mare General ... ... ,,		4 46 ,,
Bridgwater ... ... ,,		5 10 ,,
Taunton ... ... ,,		5 28 ,,
Exeter (St. David's) ... ... ,,		6 10 ,,
Dawlish ... ... ,,		6 32 ,,
Teignmouth ... ... ,,		6 40 ,,
Newton Abbot ... ... ,,		6 52 ,,
Torre ... ... ,,		7 13 ,,
Torquay ... ... ,,		7 17 ,,
Paignton ... ... ,,		7 25 ,,

A—Seats can be reserved in advance on payment of a fee of 1s. 0d. per seat (see page 30).

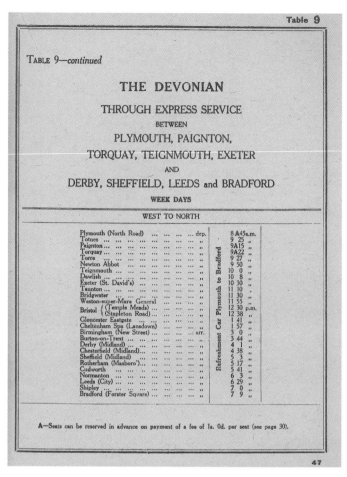

Table 9

TABLE 9—continued

THE DEVONIAN

THROUGH EXPRESS SERVICE

BETWEEN

PLYMOUTH, PAIGNTON, TORQUAY, TEIGNMOUTH, EXETER

AND

DERBY, SHEFFIELD, LEEDS and BRADFORD

WEEK DAYS

WEST TO NORTH

Plymouth (North Road) ... ... dep.		8 A45 a.m.
Totnes ... ... ,,		9 25 ,,
Paignton ... ... ,,		9A15 ,,
Torquay ... ... ,,		9A22 ,,
Torre ... ... ,,		9 27 ,,
Newton Abbot ... ... ,,		9 50 ,,
Teignmouth ... ... ,,		10 0 ,,
Dawlish ... ... ,,		10 8 ,,
Exeter (St. David's) ... ... ,,		10 30 ,,
Taunton ... ... ,,		11 10 ,,
Bridgwater ... ... ,,		11 30 ,,
Weston-super-Mare General ... ... ,,		11 55 ,,
Bristol { (Temple Meads) ... ... ,,		12 30 p.m.
Bristol { (Stapleton Road)... ... ... ,,		12 38 ,,
Gloucester Eastgate ... ... ,,		1 41 ,,
Cheltenham Spa (Lansdown) ... ... ,,	Refreshment Car Plymouth to Bradford	1 57 ,,
Birmingham (New Street) ... ... arr.		3 0 ,,
Burton-on-Trent ... ... ,,		3 44 ,,
Derby (Midland) ... ... ,,		4 1 ,,
Chesterfield (Midland)... ... ... ,,		4 38 ,,
Sheffield (Midland) ... ... ,,		5 3 ,,
Rotherham (Masbro')... ... ... ,,		5 17 ,,
Cudworth ... ... ,,		5 41 ,,
Normanton ... ... ,,		6 3 ,,
Leeds (City) ... ... ,,		6 29 ,,
Shipley ... ... ,,		7 0 ,,
Bradford (Forster Square) ... ... ,,		7 9 ,,

A—Seats can be reserved in advance on payment of a fee of 1s. 0d. per seat (see page 30).

An extract from the Western Region 1953–54 timetable showing the timings for 'The Devonian' inter-regional express which travelled over the metals of four BR regions. Strangely, this train seems to have served Plymouth only in the northbound direction.

An unwelcome interloper? Generally speaking in Devon former Great Western Railway locomotives worked the WR lines while former Southern Railway engines were confined to the SR routes. There were, however, some exceptions to this rule, especially on the Ilfracombe line, and both routes between Exeter and Plymouth where 'foreign' motive power was especially rostered for route familiarisation purposes. Here, Bulleid 'West Country' Pacific No.34030 *Watersmeet* is depicted at Newton Abbot heading for Plymouth some time in the 1950s. *Colin Hogg*

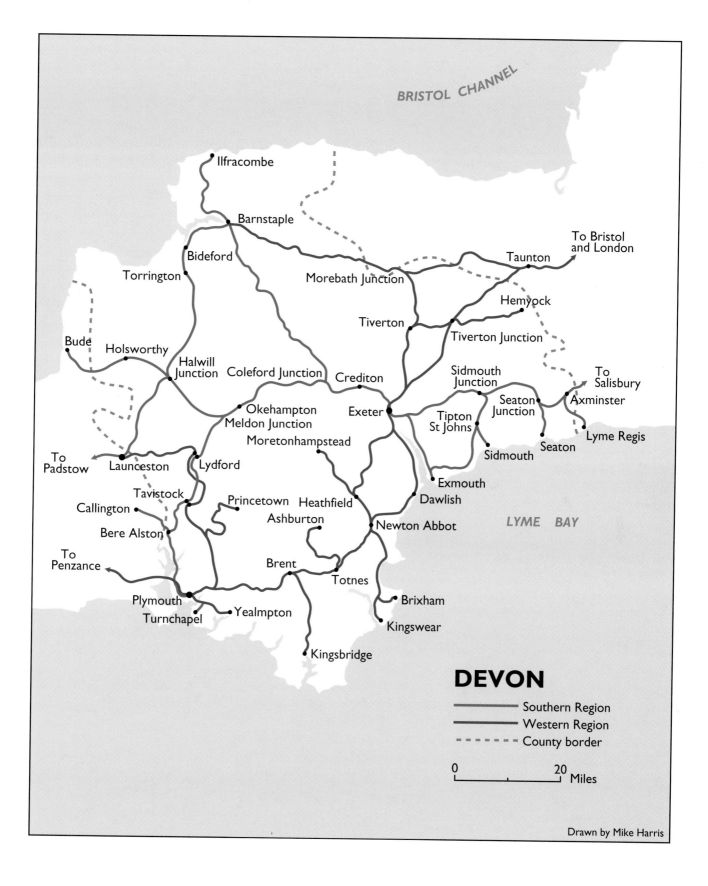

BRISTOL CHANNEL

Ilfracombe

Barnstaple

To Bristol
and London

Bideford

Taunton

Torrington

Morebath Junction

Hemyock

Tiverton

Bude

Holsworthy

Tiverton Junction

Halwill
Junction

Coleford Junction

Crediton

Sidmouth
Junction

To
Salisbury

Seaton
Junction

Axminster

Okehampton
Meldon Junction

Exeter

Tipton
St Johns

Moretonhampstead

Sidmouth

Seaton

Lyme Regis

To
Padstow

Launceston

Lydford

Exmouth

Tavistock

Dawlish

Callington

Princetown

Heathfield

LYME BAY

Ashburton

Bere Alston

Newton Abbot

To
Penzance

Brent

Plymouth

Totnes

Turnchapel

Yealmpton

Brixham

Kingswear

Kingsbridge

DEVON

——————— Southern Region

——————— Western Region

– – – – – County border

0   20 Miles

Drawn by Mike Harris

5

Lofty chimneys, gables and a fine display of BR notice boards dominate this view of the attractive frontage of Axminster station which was taken on 14th July 1960. A BR lorry is parked by the station entrance, no doubt collecting or delivering holiday-makers' luggage. The station was designed by Sir William Tite, the Gothic style and prominent chimneys being standard features of stations on the Salisbury to Exeter line. The station was opened on 19th July 1860 and almost became a junction in 1864 when a branch line to Bridport was proposed. However, it had to wait until the 20th century before junction status was achieved when the line to Lyme Regis opened for business in 1903. During the ensuing years few changes occurred but in the 1930s the down platform was lengthened to accommodate eight coaches. The Salisbury to Exeter route was transferred to the WR in 1963, and by 1967 its policy of retrenchment was in full swing and it decided to single the main line. Axminster signal box was closed from 5th March while full single line working was introduced on 11th June with all trains using the down platform, the footbridge and waiting shed on the up platform being demolished. Today Axminster has a good service with a regular flow of commuters to Exeter and double track has recently been reinstated through the station. What a turnaround! *R.C. Riley*

BRITISH TRANSPORT COMMISSION
BRITISH RAILWAYS   B.R. 21714/34

AXMINSTER

A scene at Seaton Junction recorded on 12th September 1959 showing a Maunsell-designed 'King Arthur' Class 4-6-0 leaving with a westbound train; the locomotive is No.30796 *Sir Dodinas le Savage*. This is the only picture of a 'King Arthur' that was submitted for publication in this album. An M7 Class 0-4-4T stands on the right between duties on the Seaton branch. No.30796 was an exile from the South Eastern Section being formerly based at Hither Green shed where it was something of a 'favourite' and always kept in exemplary condition, but by the time of this photograph it was in a rather grubby state. The London & South Western Railway (LSWR) received its Act of Parliament to construct the Yeovil to Exeter line on 21st July 1856 and the line was opened for traffic on 19th July 1860. *Ken Wightman / David Clark collection*

This view of Seaton Junction station was taken on 5th September 1964 and shows a very dirty Bulleid 'Battle of Britain' Class Pacific, No.34109 *Sir Trafford Leigh-Mallory*, leaving in charge of the 8.30am Padstow to Waterloo express which is about to pass the splendidly tall LSWR bracket signal that dominated this end of the station. This was the last weekday of regular steam passenger operation on the Waterloo to Exeter route and the following day No.34109 powered one of the final expresses on this line booked for steam haulage. In times past Seaton Junction station suffered from a very inconvenient layout because trains to and from Seaton had to use a west-facing bay platform which necessitated time-consuming reversals, but in 1928 the premises were entirely reconstructed with two new through tracks for main line services and a new down platform to accommodate the branch trains. *David Clark*

The line between Yeovil and Exeter was not without its challenges for enginemen in the steam era because of the heavily graded nature of the route. Westbound trains faced a three miles-long climb at 1 in 80 up to a summit just before Hewish Crossing, while shortly after departure from Axminster a much more demanding obstacle lay in their path, the almost seven mile climb, also at 1 in 80, up to a summit just beyond the western portal of Honiton tunnel. It was no easier for eastbound trains which faced longer climbs, but at least the grades were less severe. Here, against a backdrop of lush Devon rolling hills, Bulleid 'West Country' Pacific No.34108 *Wincanton* pounds up Honiton bank in charge of an express bound for the West Country on 1st June 1963. The fireman appears to be doing his job perfectly: there is barely a trace of smoke from the locomotive's chimney, indicating excellent combustion. *Rodney Lissenden*

An eastbound Exeter to Salisbury local train drifts out of Honiton tunnel behind Maunsell S15 4-6-0 No.30841 on the same day that the previous picture was taken. The first of the S15 Class appeared in 1920, being designed by Urie for the LSWR, and a further batch was constructed to Maunsell's revised specification, the first entering service in March 1927. There were considerable differences between the two batches, the Urie engines, for example, had the running board raised over the cylinders, and a different type of cab. The Maunsell engines had higher boiler pressure, reduced diameter cylinders and a modified tender design. No.30841 entered traffic in July 1936 and was withdrawn from service in January 1964; it is one of a number of these machines to have survived into preservation. *Rodney Lissenden*

Dugald Drummond's T9 Class 4-4-0s were lovely, handsome machines and, at least in the author's opinion, one of the most well-proportioned designs ever produced. A total of 66 of these elegant engines was produced between 1899 and 1901 for working express passenger trains and, as a result of their prodigious free-steaming capacity and wonderful turn of speed, were universally known as 'Greyhounds'. Construction was shared between the LSWR's works at Nine Elms (Eastleigh works had not yet been built) and Dubs & Co. of Glasgow. The T9s did not last long on front-line work, however, being largely displaced by more modern traction in the 1920s, but they were rebuilt by Urie with superheaters, larger diameter cylinders and higher boiler pressure and took on the role of secondary express locomotives, in which they excelled. Towards the end of their careers the T9 Class engines were widely spread across the South Western Section with Eastleigh and Exmouth Junction sheds having the lion's share in the late 1950s, but examples could also be found at Bournemouth, Fratton and Salisbury depots. On paper, a total of thirteen of these fine locomotives was still in traffic at the start of 1961 but some machines were stored unserviceable while other engines only worked sporadically. No.30313 was certainly still in traffic in June working from Okehampton sub-shed, and No.30117 was observed in mid-June on the 12.50pm Eastleigh to Wimborne passenger train but was clearly in bad shape and had to be assisted. On 24th June it failed completely whilst powering a local van train and apparently never worked again. The last five representatives of the class at Exmouth Junction, Nos.30120, 30313, 30709/15/17, arrived at Eastleigh works at about the same time and, apart from No.30120 retained for special duties, were withdrawn from service. It seems that the last engine to be officially withdrawn was actually No.30287 which had been in open store at Eastleigh shed since the end of the 1959 summer timetable. The spotlessly clean locomotive depicted here is No.30712, a Dubs & Co. product dating from June 1899; it is seen 'on shed' at Exmouth Junction on 5th July 1957. No.30712 lasted in service until November of the following year. *R.C. Riley*

A scene at the east end of Exeter Central station showing Maunsell Z Class 0-8-0T No.30952 which was one of eight of this class built at Brighton works in 1929 for heavy yard shunting. Apart from their quite rare wheel arrangement, these engines were immediately recognised by the footplate being raised over the cylinders, short sloping side tanks and very deep front buffer beams. Perhaps surprisingly, in the early 1950s the small class was very widely distributed across the SR with one example stationed at each of Ashford, Brighton, Three Bridges, Salisbury and Exmouth Junction sheds. The remaining three members of the class were based at Eastleigh, presumably for shunting the large marshalling yard at that location. Towards the end of their careers, however, the whole class was stationed at Exmouth Junction shed, largely for banking duties between the two main Exeter stations. One of Exeter Central station's two signal boxes can be seen on the right of the shot whilst both of the main through platforms are also discernible. This photograph was taken on 5th July 1961, No.30952's last full year of service. It was withdrawn in November 1962 but it is recorded that it survived for a further two years and was not cut-up until January 1965. *R.C. Riley*

BRITISH RAILWAYS — Southern Region

TO   787/86

EXETER CENTRAL

Exeter St David's station is located on the flood plain of the river Exe but the city centre, and Exeter Central station, is on much higher ground to the east. The Bristol & Exeter Railway (B&ER) had reached Exeter in 1844 and sixteen years elapsed before the LSWR's line from Yeovil reached the city, trains terminating at Queen Street station (later known as Exeter Central). The 50 chains-long connection between the two Exeter stations was authorised in 1860 and opened on 1st February 1862. The topography of the area made a very steep climb between the stations inevitable, the gradient being 1 in 37, one of the steepest main line inclines in Great Britain and one, moreover, nearly always tackled from a standing start in Exeter St David's station. It was therefore imperative that, if rain had made the rail surfaces greasy, locomotives had sanding gear that was working properly otherwise they could easily slither to a halt halfway up the incline. The banking duties were performed for many years by former London, Brighton & South Coast Railway E1/R Class 0-6-2Ts, latterly Nos.32124/35 and 32697, but these had probably totally exhausted themselves by 1959 and were withdrawn from traffic. They were superseded by Maunsell Z Class 0-8-0Ts and on occasions three of these machines could be seen assisting a particularly heavy train up the hill – a true display of raw steam power. The Z Class engines did not last long on this task, however, due to their boilers being life expired, and they were replaced by W Class 2-6-4Ts. This shot, taken on 23rd June 1962, shows Z Class No.30957 pushing mightily at the rear of an eastbound train hauled by Bulleid 'Battle of Britain' Pacific No.34068 *Kenley*. The meandering river Exe can just be seen on the right. *R.C. Riley*

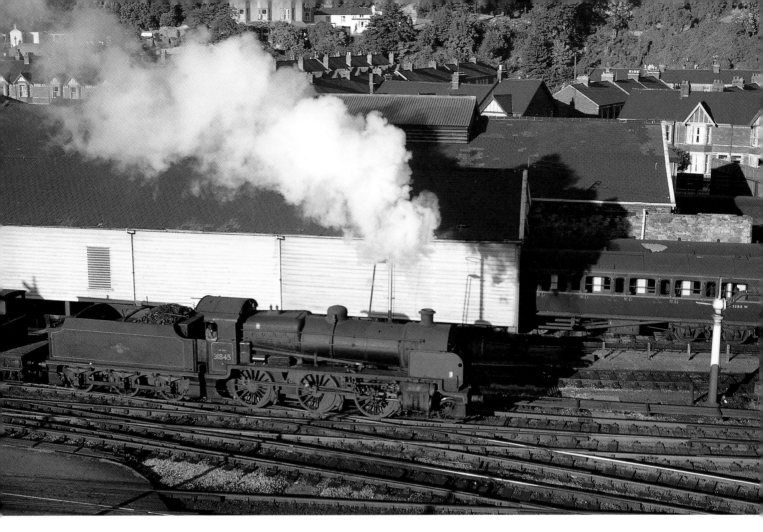

Pictured in bright sunshine, a reasonably clean Maunsell N Class 'Mogul', No.31845, has just passed through St David's station and takes the Exeter Central line on the same day that the previous picture was taken. In July 1962 Exmouth Junction locomotive shed, which was the 'Southern' shed serving the city, had a massive total of thirty N Class locomotives on its books, predictably including the machine seen here. No.31845 was built at Ashford works and entered traffic in September 1924; it was destined to remain in service for exactly 40 years, being withdrawn in September 1964. While railway enthusiasts were enthralled by the sight and sound of trains ascending the bank up to Exeter Central station one wonders how the nearby local residents reacted to the constant noise and whether they ever complained to BR. *R.C. Riley*

BRITISH TRANSPORT COMMISSION
BRITISH RAILWAYS   BR 21716/326

EXETER

The 6¾ miles-long branch from Axminster to Lyme Regis is probably one of the best-known featured in this album by virtue of the fact that for many years it was operated by a trio of Adams 'Radial' tank locomotives specially retained to work the lightly-laid and tightly-curved line. A branch from Axminster to Lyme Regis was authorised way back in 1871 but the powers lapsed and a Light Railway Order was eventually obtained in 1899 by the Axminster & Lyme Regis Light Railway Company. The line opened on 24th August 1903 but the hopes of the promoters were not realised and revenues were disappointing, resulting in the LSWR, who had worked the line from the outset, taking over completely on 1st January 1907. The branch's numerous very tight curves, steep inclines and severe weight restriction presented the LSWR with the problem of finding suitable motive power and at first LBSCR 'Terriers' were employed, but by 1905 traffic was so heavy that O2 Class 0-4-4Ts were drafted to the route and these machines took over entirely in 1907, having to run with only partly filled tanks to reduce their weight. In 1914 Adams 'Radial' tank locomotive Nos.125, 419 and 521 were tried out on the branch and proved an immediate success, and to reduce tyre wear their bogies were modified to give extra side play to make the engines more suitable for the tight curves. By 1928 the 'Radial' tank locomotives were the only survivors of their class in SR stock and in need of heavy repair, so the Southern Railway experimented with former SECR P Class 0-6-0T No.A558 and former LBSCR D1 Class 0-4-2T No.B612. The latter proved to be more suitable than the P Class engine and four examples were modified for use on the branch and sent to Exmouth Junction shed, but in practice they were found to be less successful than anticipated and it was decided to undertake extensive repairs to the Adams locomotives which were languishing at Eastleigh works. The 'Radial' tank locomotives subsequently monopolised services along the branch for many years, but in 1946 both locomotives needed repairs and it was decided to purchase sister engine No.488, then in the stock of the East Kent Railway. Following nationalisation the three Adams 'Radial' locomotives were re-numbered, becoming Nos.30582/83/84, and were based at Exmouth Junction shed for use on the Lyme Regis branch, but in 1958 their supremacy was challenged again when WR Class 1400 0-4-2T No.1462 was given a trial on the branch with unfortunate results. This locomotive not only lost time on the line's steep banks but also damaged the permanent way so No.1462 was returned to its home shed in disgrace. The beautifully proportioned Adams locomotives were eventually replaced in early 1961 by Ivatt-designed 2-6-2Ts following track alterations but the latter did not last long, being soon ousted by diesel units; however the Ivatt tank engines did make a brief re-appearance in 1965 when the WR (who controlled the lines west of Salisbury by that time) was short of diesel units. Alas, traffic on the line was largely seasonal and regular customers during the wintertime were few and far between, and the inconvenient location of Lyme Regis station, perched 250ft above sea level, no doubt contributed to the line's downfall. The passenger service was withdrawn in November 1965, the line closing completely from that date when the south of England lost one of its most delightful branch lines. Lyme Regis trains started from a bay platform at Axminster located on the north side of the main line and were immediately faced with a sharp 1 in 80 climb round a tight curve to cross over the main line on a bridge. In this picture, taken on 18th June 1960, Adams 'Radial' tank locomotive No.30583 sits in Axminster station before taking out a train to Lyme Regis. In contrast to the somewhat dilapidated water tank, and footbridge which is partially visible on the right, the locomotive appears to be lovingly cared for. Officially withdrawn in July 1961, No.30583 was lucky enough to find a new home on the Bluebell Railway where it can still be seen, although it is not currently operational. *Roy Denison*

The Lyme Regis branch, as previously mentioned, was monopolised by the elegant 'Adams' Radial locomotives whose short coupled wheelbase made them ideal motive power for a line infested with tight curves. In this picture, taken from the front coach of a train bound for Lyme Regis on 14th May 1960, No.30582 negotiates a sharp bend in the track between Axminster and Combpyne. *John Langford*

A charming scene on the Lyme Regis branch. Despite a lot of cloud in the sky, the sun was shining at just the right moment as No.30582 bursts out from behind a line of trees and creates a really evocative picture, recalling the heyday of this much-loved branch. The identity of the train is unknown but the main-line Bulleid carriages, and the fact that engines normally worked chimney first towards Lyme Regis, suggest a through working from London Waterloo. This picture is thought to have been taken in 1956. *Colin Hogg*

Combpyne was the only intermediate station on the branch and in this picture Ivatt-designed Class 2MT 2-6-2T No.41318 is seen pulling away from the station with a train bound for Lyme Regis on 6th July 1961. This station was a crossing point at one time but the loop line connection at the Axminster end was removed in 1930, thus creating a siding where a camping coach was stationed for many years. The platform at Combpyne was totally devoid of any shelter – the station building is located adjacent to a nearby road – so joining a train on a wet and windy night must have been an experience to remember! Apart from a short 1 in 200 section, after leaving Combpyne workings bound for Lyme Regis had all the inclines in their favour and could coast all the way to the terminus, thus giving the fireman a well-earned breather. *R.C. Riley*

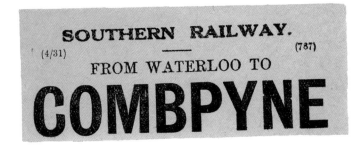

Table 38					AXMINSTER and LYME REGIS																							
Miles	**Down**							**Week Days**																					
		SO	SX	SO	SO	SX	SO			SX	SO	SX	SO	SX	SO	SO	pm		SX	SO	M	FO	SO						
	Axminster . . dep	8 32	8 43	9 35	1035	1040	11C35	. .	1233	1243	1 38	1050	2 48	3 40	4A42	4 42	5 40	6 45	6 50	8 55	9 15	9Y45	1045						
4¾	Combpyne	8 45	8 56	9 48	1048	1053	11C48	. . .	1246	1256	1 51	20	3 13	3 53	4A55	4 55	5 53	6 58	7 3	9 8	9 28	. . . .	. . . .						
6¾	Lyme Regis . . arr	8 53	9 4	9 56	1056	11 1	11C56	. .	1254	4 1	59	2011	3 9	4	5A 3	5	6 1	7 6	7 11	9 16	9 36	10Y11	11 3						
Miles	**Up**							**Week Days**																					
		am	SO	SX			SO	SX	SO			SX	SO			SX	SO	SX	SO	pm			pm	pm					
	Lyme Regis . . dep	7Y29	8 0	8 11	. .	9E 0	10 0	10 5	. .	11 5	1183	1210	. .	1 101	12	. .	2 16	3F 5	3 53	4 10	5 10	. .	6 7	8 22					
2¼	Combpyne	. . . .	8 8	8 19	. . .	9E 8	10 8	1013	. . .	1113	1184	5 1218	. . .	1 18	1 20	. .	2 24	3F 13	4	1 14	18	5 18	. .	6 15	8 30				
6¾	Axminster . . arr	7Y55	8 21	8 32	. .	9E21	1021	1026	. .	1126	1185	8 1231	. .	1 31	1 33	. .	2 37	3F 26	4	14 4	31	5 31	. .	6 28	8 43				
	Down				**Sundays**								**Up**					**Sundays**											
		am	am	pm	pm	pm	pm	pm	pm	pm	pm	pm				am	am	pm	pm	pm	pm	pm	pm	pm				
	Axminster . . . . dep	11 11	12 6	1 0	220	320	425	550	716	816	922	1025	Lyme Regis . . dep			1040	1137	1233	1 48	2 50	3 55	456	645	744	850	9 55		
	Combpyne	. . . .	1124	1219	113	233	333	438	6	3	729	829	935	1038	Combpyne		1048	1145	1241	1 56	2 58	4	3	5 4	653	752	858	10 3	
	Lyme Regis . . . arr	1132	1227	121	241	341	446	61	1	737	837	946	1046	Axminster . . . arr		11	1158	1254	2	9 3	11 4	16	517	7	6	8 5	9 11	1016

A Through Carriages from Waterloo, dep 1 0 pm. (Table 31.)   B Through Carriages to Waterloo, arr 3 40 pm. (Table 31.)
C Through Carriages from Waterloo, dep 8 5 am, until 24th August. (Table 31.)   D Through Carriages from Waterloo,
dep 10 45 am. (Table 31.)   E Through Carriages to Waterloo, arr 12 36 pm, 29th June to 7th September (Table 31.)
F Through Carriages to Waterloo, arr 6 38 pm. (Table 31.)   FO Fridays only.   M Mondays to Thursdays and Saturdays,
SO Saturdays only.   SX Mondays to Fridays.   Y By Southern National Omnibus between Axminster Station and Lyme
Regis: 7 29 am departs from Lyme Regis Station. Times subject to alteration.

Southern Region 1957 summer timetable

Cows graze contentedly in the field on the left of the shot as a train bound for Lyme Regis, hauled by Adams 'Radial' locomotive No.30582, leaves Cannington viaduct and coasts downhill towards its destination. Southbound trains approached the viaduct on a falling gradient of 1 in 40, which is clearly visible in the picture, but this eases to 1 in 82 across the viaduct, whilst later the falling grades vary between 1 in 55 and 1 in 94, so the drivers who worked the line certainly needed to have their wits about them, and their hand on the engine's brake valve, at the appropriate moment! The ten-arch viaduct is 203 yards-long, the maximum height above the valley being 93ft, and it is the only engineering work of any consequence on the branch. The appearance of the structure has always been spoiled to some degree by its drooped look at one end, this being a legacy of subsidence that occurred during building. This necessitated a jack arch in the third span to prevent further settlement, but this essential feature also mars the appearance of the viaduct. This picture is also believed to have been taken in 1956. *Colin Hogg*

LYME REGIS BRANCH

The 4¼ miles-long branch from Seaton Junction, on the main line from London to Exeter, to the small seaside resort of Seaton was authorised on 13th July 1863 and opened on 16th March 1868. The Seaton & Beer Railway was always worked by the LSWR and in 1887 the latter absorbed the local company which had originally proposed the line. The name Beer in the title refers to the fishing village of that name to the west of Seaton. The line ran through Colyton and Colyford to a station at Seaton located on the west bank of the river Axe but Beer was not directly served. There were some steep 1 in 76 climbs on the line but these are unlikely to have troubled enginemen, the usual branch trains being a mere two coaches. In the summer months Seaton was quite a busy station and in the summer of 1959 3,500 tickets were issued and 12,000 collected and, of course, there would have been other passengers using holiday runabout tickets. In the late 1950s through portions to and from Waterloo were generally provided on three separate services. Sadly, the branch's buoyant traffic during the short summer period was insufficient to stave off closure, which occurred on 7th March 1966, but it is still possible to travel along the bank of the river Axe from Seaton to Colyton on a tramway which occupies part of the route of the former line. In this picture M7 Class 0-4-4T No.30021 is seen shunting (what appears to be) the Seaton portion of a London-bound train at Seaton Junction station on 12th September 1959. *R.C.Riley*

The 1928 rebuilding of Seaton Junction station involved, as previously mentioned, the provision of a new down platform which obviated the need for branch trains to reverse into and out of the station. For years LSWR M7 Class 0-4-4Ts were the customary motive power for Seaton branch services and these lasted until the early 1960s when DMUs took over. In early 1965, however, the WR experienced an acute shortage of DMUs and the unit operating the Seaton branch was commandeered for use elsewhere on the region. Much to the amazement of the railway enthusiast fraternity from 15th February 1965 a revised timetable was introduced, the last two remaining 1400 Class 0-4-2Ts, Nos.1442 and 1450, having been drafted across from Yeovil to Exmouth Junction shed to operate the branch with auto trailers. Only one locomotive was required at a time, however, the other remaining 'spare' at Exmouth Junction. Here, No.1450 is seen standing in the branch platform at Seaton Junction station on 13th February 1965 with a small group of passengers, who look suspiciously like railway enthusiasts, standing on the platform. This shot was taken two days before the new timetable came into effect – perhaps the train depicted was undergoing a trial run. The unexpected appearance of the 1400 Class engines and auto trailers on the Seaton branch proved to be the swansong for this traditional form of GWR operation – and on a former 'Southern' line at that!
Roy Denison

Somewhere across the fields an engine was heard puffing along. 1400 Class 0-4-2T No.1450, apparently propelling an auto coach, slowly makes its way along the Seaton branch with the Devon landscape looking appealing even in wintertime. No.1450 was built at Swindon works in July 1935 and was subsequently preserved. A February 1965 picture.
Roy Denison

Sidmouth is a classic holiday town and at one time was reputed to have more four-star hotels than any other equivalent resort on the south coast. The first railway to the town was proposed way back in 1862 but the scheme was later abandoned despite preliminary works being undertaken. The plans were revived in 1871 and a new Act was obtained, and on 6th July 1874 the branch, which left the Salisbury to Exeter line near the village of Feniton, was opened to traffic. It was characterised by some very fierce gradients, some as steep as 1 in 45, and also beautiful south Devon countryside especially along the valley of the river Otter. The main line station was, naturally enough, named Sidmouth Junction. In 1863 a line from Sidmouth to the prosperous coastal resort of Budleigh Salterton had been authorised but construction of such a route was clearly impracticable due to the extremely severe gradients needed and the powers lapsed. The next development was in 1894 when a line was agreed from Tipton St Johns (3¼ miles from Sidmouth) to Budleigh Salterton and this was opened on 15th May 1897, more than 30 years after the first plans were made. The following year saw an extension to Exmouth authorised, this opening on 1st June 1903. The Sidmouth Railway always managed to retain its independence, although the line was worked by the LSWR, but the Tipton St Johns-Budleigh Salterton-Exmouth line was always directly owned by the LSWR. All of the aforementioned routes lost their passenger services from 6th March 1967, including Sidmouth Junction station, but the latter was re-opened as Feniton in May 1971, no doubt in response to considerable building development that had taken place since closure. Sidmouth station consisted of an island platform accommodating seven coaches on one side and five on the other and such a cramped and restricted layout caused problems; long trains had to be divided by a locomotive provided especially for that purpose. In this view Ivatt Class 2MT 2-6-2T No.41306 is depicted standing in Sidmouth station on 13th July 1960 at the head of (what appears to be) a very long van train. It is unlikely that such a train would have been needed for passengers' luggage, so this is presumably a special working of some sort. At one time there was a considerable amount of inwards coal traffic to the local gasworks and even after this was closed substantial domestic coal traffic continued for some years.
R.C. Riley

SIDMOUTH BRANCH

The locomotive seen in the previous shot is depicted at the country end of Sidmouth station on the same day. The signalman looks down from his tall LSWR-pattern box and appears to be in conversation with the shunter standing on the ground by the side of the engine's front buffer beam. Note the brightly coloured regulation fire buckets beneath the signal box steps. The huge sign on the front of the signalbox is very prominent, but how many passengers would have spotted a sign displayed at such a height? *R.C. Riley*

A picture of Topsham station, looking northwards, in the late 1950s. The main station building is the work of the eminent architect Sir William Tite who designed some notable railway buildings. Topsham station was most unusual because the line northwards to Exmouth Junction was converted to double track at about the time of the First World War due to increasing traffic, but the rest of the route remained single. There was a reasonably-sized goods yard with a goods shed on the down side of the line. A little-known feature of the railway at Topsham was a 700 yards-long branch to a wharf on the river Exe which opened on 23rd September 1861 and lasted until 1957, the track being lifted during the following year. *Stuart Ackley collection*

Prior to the opening of the railway to Exmouth the usual route for passengers travelling from Exeter to Exmouth was via the South Devon Railway to Starcross from where they were taken by ferry across the river Exe to Exmouth. On 2nd July 1855 the Exeter & Exmouth Railway obtained an Act of Parliament to construct a broad gauge link from Exminster to Exmouth but, not surprisingly, nothing came of this unrealistic proposal due to the enormous cost of building a bridge across the estuary of the river Exe. In 1858 the Exeter & Exmouth Company reached an agreement with the LSWR and obtained an amendment to its original Act, the outcome being that the latter company would build a standard gauge line from a point 1¼ miles east of Exeter to Topsham and the independent company would complete the line to Exmouth. The entire line was opened on 1st May 1861 and five years later the local company was absorbed by the LSWR. In this picture BR Standard Class 3MT 2-6-2T No.82025 skirts the Exe estuary near Lympstone with the 2.15pm Exeter Central to Exmouth train on 13th October 1959. *R.C. Riley*

A bird's-eye view of the Exeter end of Exmouth station on the same day as the previous picture showing M7 Class 0-4-4T No.30676 apparently running-round after arriving from Exeter. The branch to Budleigh Salterton can just be glimpsed between the signal box and houses on the left of the picture. The impressive 70-lever signal box dated from the reconstruction of the station that was planned by the LSWR but actually carried out by the Southern Railway in 1924/25. The new station had a glazed concourse, four platforms, bookstall and impressive office block surmounted by a clock and the frequent train service gave the place the air of a commuter station – there were even extra trains during the peak! Goods services over the branch to Budleigh Salterton ceased in 1964 and the line was closed completely in March 1967. Goods facilities were withdrawn from the Exmouth branch in December of that year. *R.C. Riley*

Southern Region 1957 summer timetable

A nicely cleaned Ivatt-designed Class 2MT 2-6-2T No.41306 awaits departure with an Exeter train at Exmouth station on 13th October 1959. Note the fine bracket signal with its lower quadrant arms that controlled this part of the station. Diesel units made their first appearance on the line in June 1963 and it was not long before they had completely ousted steam traction on passenger work, the engine shed, which was a sub-shed of Exmouth Junction, closing from 4th November 1963. There used to be a short line to Exmouth docks, on which speed was restricted to 4mph, and all shunting operations were accompanied by a pilotman with a red flag; this line was closed in December 1967. *R.C. Riley*

EXMOUTH BRANCH

The county border between Devon and Somerset runs across the top of the Blackdown Hills which the Taunton to Exeter line cuts through in Whiteball tunnel. Eastbound trains face a gradual climb to Whiteball summit mostly at 1 in 115 or thereabouts, but those heading westwards have to contend with three miles at about 1 in 86, a much tougher proposition. In this photograph, taken on 18th July 1959, 'Modified Hall' Class 4-6-0 No.6960 *Raveningham Hall* has just passed the summit close to Whiteball siding signal box, so the hard work is over for the crew who can now coast downhill towards Tiverton Junction. The train reporting number identifies the 7.40am Paddington to Paignton, a dated working that ran on Saturdays only from 4th July to 29th August. *R.C. Riley*

An old style running-in board on the right, a GWR-designed signal box and typical lower quadrant signals, plus a complete train of pre-nationalisation carriages ... this could, at first glance, almost be mistaken for a precious colour photograph taken in GWR days. This scene was photographed at Stoke Canon, between Tiverton Junction and Exeter, on 6th July 1957 and depicts the 10.35am SO Paignton to Wolverhampton (Low Level) train which was routed via Stratford-upon-Avon; motive power is provided by Collett-designed 'Grange' Class 4-6-0 No.6829 *Burmington Grange*, a Swindon product dating from March 1937. Stoke Canon station was closed from 13th June 1960. In the days before cheap continental holidays became the norm for the masses, most British families spent their annual summer holiday at the seaside and, of course, Devon was one of the most popular destinations. Unfortunately from the railway authorities' point of view the annual exodus was determined to a large degree by the dates of the school holidays and, as a result, a huge number of people took their holiday during the peak months of July and August. This put a tremendous strain on the railway's resources as it endeavoured to cope with crowds of holiday-makers, and sets of coaches were retained specially to cater for this traffic. During the Beeching era this type of traffic was seen to be completely uneconomic and trains such as this quickly became a thing of the past. The train seen here was just one of a large number of Saturday holiday trains run between Paignton and the West Midlands at this time – there was even a Fridays-only overnight service! *R.C. Riley*

G. W. R.

STOKE CANON

TAUNTON TO EXETER

A view of Tiverton Junction station, looking southwards, on 23rd August 1964. This station, which had two fast lines with loops serving both the up and down platforms, was situated on the main line from Taunton to Exeter which came into use in 1844. The branch to Tiverton is out of sight on the right of the picture while the branch line to Hemyock diverged on the down side. Note the attractive floral displays on the down platform and typical BR 'sausage' station signs of that period. The locomotive carrying out some shunting was probably 'playing to the gallery', because a group of railway enthusiasts (some of whom are visible on the platform) had just returned from a journey down the delightful line to Hemyock. The trip had been specially arranged by the Tiverton Junction stationmaster, Fred Pugh, for a group of his friends, and involved the use of former GWR 1400 Class 0-4-2T, No.1450, which is puffing about the station area. By the date of this photograph the branch had been diesel-worked for some time and this is thought to have been the last time steam traction penetrated to Hemyock. This station seen here was closed in May 1986 and replaced by the nearby Tiverton Parkway station and almost everything of railway interest in this picture has since been erased from the landscape. *John Langford*

Tiverton Junction station was typical of many railway junctions where a large station, without much originating traffic of its own, had been built when the railways were at the height of their prosperity in Victorian times, almost solely to enable passengers to change onto branch line services. The station was actually situated in the village of Willand and nearby settlements included Halberton, Sampford Peverell and Uffculme, all of which had stations of their own so their inhabitants are unlikely to have used Tiverton Junction. This shot gives an idea of the scale of this quite large station which was controlled by a huge signal box on the up platform. A glance at the 1954/55 winter timetable reveals that only a few fast main line trains bothered to stop, the majority of the services on the main line that called being purely local trains between Taunton and Exeter. In this picture, taken on 7th August 1961, a 1400 Class 0-4-2T is seen pottering around the station environs in between duties on the Hemyock branch. *Roy Denison*

Decline of Western Steam. By the summer of 1963 diesel traction was well established on WR front-line services and steam locomotives, which were in an increasingly parlous condition, were relegated to relatively menial tasks. Substantial inroads were being made into the much-loved GWR-designed steam classes and, indeed, by this time all of the legendary 'King' Class 4-6-0s had gone and for many enthusiasts the WR would never be quite the same again. By way of compensation, a large number of 'Castle' Class 4-6-0s remained at work and these included No.5098 *Clifford Castle* which is seen here passing Cowley Bridge Junction with an Exeter to Paddington van train on 2nd June 1963 – hardly a prestigious working. No.5098 was destined to survive for exactly another year in service before being consigned to the scrap yard. *Rodney Lissenden*

The 'King' Class 4-6-0s, a Collett design that first appeared in 1927, were the most powerful locomotives in Great Britain when they were introduced, and were built up to the maximum axle loading allowed on the GWR system. These 89-ton machines had four cylinders and produced a 40,285lb. tractive effort, and enabled the GWR to regain its position as the company possessing the most powerful locomotives which had been lost to the Southern Railway, with their recently introduced 'Lord Nelson' Class. The 'Kings' had very limited route availability due to their excessive weight and were only permitted to work between Paddington and Plymouth or Wolverhampton via Bicester. In this shot No.6018 *King Henry VI* is seen approaching Cowley Bridge Junction, just north of Exeter, with an eastbound, morning train of mixed rolling stock which includes pre-nationalisation and BR Standard designs in a variety of liveries. All of the impressive 'King' Class engines were withdrawn from service in 1962 but, despite being officially withdrawn in December of that year, *King Henry VI* was specially retained to work a commemorative rail tour in April 1963, so became the last of its class to work in the BR steam era. *R.C. Riley*

TAUNTON TO EXETER

The former Great Western Railway was famed for the immense pride it took in its locomotive fleet, especially the express passenger locomotives that were more in the public eye. This is exemplified here by the absolutely immaculate condition of 'Castle' Class 4-6-0 No.5029 *Nunney Castle* which is seen here at Exeter St David's station in charge of an up express on 24th April 1960. Note the shining copper-capped chimney, motion and tender frame – whoever cleaned this engine did a very thorough job. Full marks to the cleaners at Laira shed! Note also the forest of lower quadrant semaphore signals which was destined to last until a re-signalling scheme was implemented in the mid-1980s. *Nunney Castle* survived into preservation so this picture might still be taken today – minus the lovely signals, of course! *Roy Denison*

The massive bulk of Exeter West signal box dominates the background of this illustration of 'Grange' Class 4-6-0 No.6827 *Llanfrechfa Grange* setting off for Newton Abbot with a goods train in tow. The historic signal box was closed in 1985 as a result of a re-signalling scheme and was carefully dismantled and re-erected at the Crewe Heritage Centre, where it can still be seen at the time of writing. Exeter city centre is situated on the hill to the left of the picture while the river Exe can be seen on the right. This photograph was taken in glorious evening sunshine on 23rd June 1962. *R.C. Riley*

A bird's-eye view of Exeter engine shed and hinterland taken on 23rd September 1962, looking northwards. Between 1844 and 1851 the Bristol & Exeter Railway (B&ER) used a small, temporary engine shed, which was replaced by a three-road building with space for 15 locomotives and remained in use until 1864. In 1846 the South Devon Railway (SDR) constructed an engine shed which was situated at the southern end of the station and this also lasted until 1864 when the station underwent extensive rebuilding. The main shed building seen here dates from the rebuilding of the station and was extended in 1894 by the GWR being rebuilt with a 'northlight' roof; a coaling stage and ramp approach were also added. This distinctive roof was presumably replaced some time after the Second World War: certainly the roof seen in this picture seems to be fairly new. Note that the coal stage is not topped by the customary water tank which has its own free-standing tank house to the left of the main shed building. Judging by the huge pile of fuel on the extreme left of the picture the depot was certainly not in danger of running out of coal, but in reality by this date it was probably using less and less as the steam fleet was in decline – note the empty roads in front of the principal shed building. The two tracks immediately to the right of the shed are the goods avoiding lines. It was a sad day when the shed closed to steam traction on 14th October 1963. *R.C .Riley*

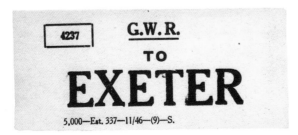

The final intermediate station on the line from Taunton to Barnstaple was Swimbridge where a very dirty 4300 Class 2-6-0, No.6343, was photographed hauling a short goods train on 24th April 1960. Unfortunately the route was quite expensive to maintain with three tunnels, viaducts and many bridges, not to mention a dozen signal boxes. There was quite heavy cattle traffic on the line at one time but this ceased in 1963 and subsequently the through goods trains were diverted to run via Exeter. When the whole branch closed to goods this left only a DMU-operated local service until the entire route was shut completely on 3rd October 1966. *Roy Denison*

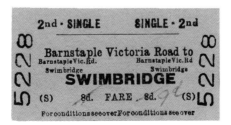

Barnstaple originally had two stations, the LSWR Barnstaple Junction station which provided services to Exeter, Ilfracombe and Torrington, and Barnstaple (Victoria Road) the former GWR station on the route to Taunton. Victoria Road was built by the Devon & Somerset Railway which obtained an Act of Parliament to construct a broad gauge line from Taunton (Norton Fitzwarren) on 29th July 1864. The company was beset by financial problems and the opening of the single track line throughout was delayed until 1st November 1873; the line was leased to the B&ER and conversion to standard gauge took place in May 1881. In 1887 a spur to the LSWR's Barnstaple Junction station was brought into use thus enabling through expresses to operate from London and the Midlands to Ilfracombe. Later, on 1st July 1905, the short Barnstaple eastern spur was opened and this enabled trains from Taunton to the North Devon coast to pass through Barnstaple without the need to reverse at Victoria Road station. In the 1930s holiday traffic to Ilfracombe was booming and various improvements were made including the doubling of the Norton Fitzwarren to Milverton section and lengthening of loops at some stations. The 1955 timetable advertised eight stopping trains in each direction between Barnstaple and Taunton but on summer Saturdays the route was much busier with five holiday trains scheduled, which stopped at only the principal stations, and there were doubtless as many unadvertised extra workings as the line capacity would permit. Victoria Road station was closed to passengers on 13th June 1960 from which date all services were concentrated on the Junction station, but it remained in use for goods purposes until 5th March 1970. This picture, looking west towards the buffer stops, was taken on 24th April 1960, not long before the station closed its doors to passengers for the last time. *Roy Denison*

A view of the country end of Barnstaple Victoria Road station on the same day as the previous shot with a former GWR 4300 Class 2-6-0 on the right. The lower quadrant semaphore signals and brown-painted running-in board certainly dispelled any doubts regarding the origins of the station. The tightly-curved spur line round to Barnstaple Junction station can just be discerned diverging in the distance. *Roy Denison*

Most trains on the Taunton to Barnstaple line terminated at Barnstaple Junction station and in this view former GWR 4300 Class 2-6-0 No.7337 is depicted pausing in the down main platform after arrival with a train from Taunton. The building visible at the end of the up platform is the goods shed with the engine shed beyond; the routes to Ilfracombe and Bideford diverged immediately behind the photographer. This photograph was taken in August 1962. *Lens of Sutton Association*

The 7¼ miles-long branch from Tiverton Junction to Hemyock was promoted by the Culm Valley Light Railway Company whose shareholders comprised local landowners and farmers. In 1873 they obtained powers under the 1868 Regulation of Railways Act to lay a cheaply-built standard gauge line with a maximum axle weight of eight tons and top speed of 15mph. Intermediate stations were initially provided at Uffculme and Culmstock and the branch opened on 29th May 1876. Unbridled optimism reigned supreme and the shareholders were no doubt disappointed when construction costs were well above budget and traffic was half that predicted; to add to their misery the line opened two years later than anticipated. The disillusioned landowners met for the last time on 2nd April 1880 and decided to sell the line to the GWR for £33,000. Passenger services were notoriously slow, the four trains each way advertised in the 1922 timetable taking between 33min and 1hr 5min for the journey, this being largely due to some notoriously tight curves and the need to halt at level crossings for the fireman to open and close the gates. In ensuing years the fortunes of the line improved somewhat with the establishment of a dairy at Hemyock and construction of a textile mill at Uffculme which proved to be the line's salvation and, indeed, the branch will be remembered best by enthusiasts for its considerable milk traffic. The very slow passenger trains were certainly not designed for those in a hurry and in later years were reckoned to be the slowest in the BR timetable – what an accolade! Passenger services ended on 7th September 1963, most residents in the valley having long deserted the railway, but goods services continued to operate until the dairy closed in October 1975 and this rural backwater quietly faded into history. Coldharbour Halt, seen here on 15th June 1962, was one of two halts on the branch opened by the GWR in the inter-war period and dated from March 1929. *R.C. Riley*

Table 83   TIVERTON JUNCTION and HEMYOCK—(Third class only)

Miles		Week Days only							Miles		Week Days only						
---	---	a.m	a.m E	a.m S	p.m	p.m	p.m	p.m	---	---	a.m	a.m	p.m E	p.m S	p.m	p.m	p.m
—	Tiverton Junction..dep	8 45	1135	1135	..	1 40	4 30	7 5	—	Hemyock..........dep	7 20	1030	..	..	3 0	5 55	7 55
2¼	Coldharbour Halt	8 54	1144	1144	..	1 48	4 38	7 14	1	Whitehall Halt	7 24	1034	..	..	3 5	6 0	8 0
2¾	Uffculme	8 57	1147	1147	..	1 52	4 42	7 17	2½	Culmstock	7 31	1043	..	1210	3 13	6 8	8 7
5	Culmstock	9 21	..	12 5	..	2 4	4 52	7 27	4½	Uffculme	7 40	1053	..	1219	3 25	6 18	8 17
6¼	Whitehall Halt	9 30	..	..	..	2 13	5 0	7 35	5	Coldharbour Halt	7 43	1057	1218	1223	3 30	6 22	8 20
7¼	Hemyock..........arr	9 42	..	..	..	2 20	5 5	7 40	7¼	Tiverton Junction..arr	7 52	11 7	1228	1233	3 41	6 33	8 29

E Except Saturdays.   S Saturdays only.

Western Region 1953–54 winter timetable

A timeless scene on the Hemyock branch. It wasn't just Small's seeds that succeeded because the Culm Valley railway also succeeded in providing the valley's residents with rail transport for both passengers and goods for almost a century. This photograph, that depicts 1400 Class 0-4-2T No.1451 leaving Uffculme with a Tiverton Junction train on 7th August 1961, beautifully encapsulates the rural nature of this quiet backwater. Some of the curves on the line had to be seen to be believed as the tracks followed the sinuous course of the river Culm. *Roy Denison*

Another picture taken at Uffculme, this time showing the design of the simple stations provided on the branch. The station is certainly tiny but has an excellent display of posters and the flower beds are really colourful. The premises appear to be equipped with gas lighting which is an improvement on the rather basic oil lamps used at other stations. Note the extremely tight curve beyond the bridge which carries the line across the river Culm. *Stuart Ackley collection*

Culmstock station, which was photographed on 11th June 1962, was built in a similar style to Uffculme but somehow does not seem quite as welcoming – perhaps it is because the sun was not shining when this shot was taken! The flower beds seem to be empty and there are only a couple of posters visible on the main building. It is recorded that the station became unmanned from 2nd May 1960 and this may account for its slightly neglected air. The middle track is a run-round loop which was used regularly once a week when the lunchtime train from Tiverton Junction to Uffculme was extended to Culmstock on Saturdays. *Gerald Daniels*

Whitehall Halt, like Coldharbour Halt seen in a previous picture, was also built in the inter-war period and in this case dated from 1932. It was clearly cheaply built in the standard 'wood and ash' style of the period, the platform being long enough to accommodate one coach and nothing more. The tiny hut at ground level on the right hand side beyond the platform appears to be a waiting shelter for passengers, or perhaps it should be passenger, because it only seems large enough to hold one person and a small amount of luggage! The shelter at Coldharbour seems commodious by comparison. The other hut was presumably a shunter's cabin from where the points were operated: note the rodding on the left of the shot. At least the gates appear to be quite freshly painted. One wonders whether this halt was the most 'basic' the GWR ever had! *Gerald Daniels*

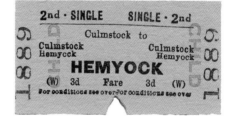

Journey's end – Hemyock station. In this illustration 1400 Class 0-4-2T No.1451 simmers beside the water crane at Hemyock on 7th August 1961 while the coach berthed in the background is one of the two five-compartment former Barry Railway gas-lit vehicles that provided the passenger accommodation on the branch for many years. They were the only carriages permitted on the branch at that time due to the very tight curves previously mentioned. Naturally, they were of considerable interest to the railway aficionados of the day, being the last gas-lit coaches on the WR; they were replaced by a couple of Thompson-designed brake second vehicles in 1962. Milk traffic from the Culm Valley Dairy Co. factory at Hemyock, just across the road from the station, kept the line in business for many years and the closure of the plant in late 1975 resulted in the charming Hemyock branch being shut too – how sad. *Roy Denison*

Gas lighting, an old barrow, blackboard notices and one of the finest collections of vintage enamel platform signs imaginable: this is the scene that greeted passengers at Tiverton station on 18th July 1964. In addition there was the train waiting at the platform, of course, an auto train working to Tiverton Junction with 1400 Class 0-4-2T No.1450 in charge. The 4½ miles-long branch from Tiverton to Tiverton Junction was the first branch line to be constructed in Devon and was opened by the B&ER on 12th June 1848. It was built as a broad gauge line with a double track formation but in the event only one track was laid; the line was converted to standard gauge in June 1884. The branch was scenically unspectacular, the only point of real interest being an aqueduct which carried the Grand Western canal across the line; this was built with separate arches for the up and down lines. Latterly, about a dozen trains were advertised in each direction on weekdays and these supposedly connected with other services at each end of the line. Let us hope that the day trippers really enjoyed their 'Sunday by the Sea' at either Exmouth or Sidmouth or, perhaps, somewhere in the Torbay area, because when this picture was taken the branch had already been sanctioned for closure and it was likely to be their very last day trip by rail from Tiverton. Passenger trains were withdrawn from 5th October 1964, outliving those on the Exe Valley line, while goods traffic lasted until June 1967. *Roy Denison*

Table 85	TIVERTON JUNCTION and TIVERTON—(Third class only)															
Miles		**Week Days**														
		a.m	a.m		a.m	a.m	a.m	a.m		p.m		p.m	p.m	p.m	p.m		p.m	p.m	
							T										
	Tiverton Junction..dep	7 25	8 15	..	9 2	9 40	1035	1135	..	1245	..	1 40	4 25	5 32	7 5	..	8 40	9 30	..
2¼	Halberton Halt........	7 31	8 20	..	9 7	9 45	1040	1140	..	1250	..	1 45	4 30	5 37	7 10	..	8 45	9 35	..
4½	Tiverton............arr	7 38	8 27	..	9 14	9 52	1047	1147	..	1257	..	1 52	4 37	5 44	7 17	..	8 52	9 42	..
Miles		**Week Days**														
		a.m	a.m		a.m	a.m	a.m		p.m	p.m		p.m	p.m	p.m	p.m		p.m	p.m	
	Tiverton............dep	7 11	7 40	..	8 45	9 20	11 5	..	1220	1 20	..	4 0	4 45	6 25	8 15	..	9 0	1040	..
2¼	Halberton Halt........	7 17	7 47	..	8 51	9 26	1111	..	1226	1 26	..	4 6	4 51	6 31	8 21	..	9 6	1046	..
4½	Tiverton Junction..arr	7 23	7 53	..	8 57	9 32	1117	..	1232	1 32	..	4 12	4 57	6 37	8 27	..	9 12	1052	..

G Commences 2nd May, 1954.   T Tuesdays only

Western Region 1953–54 winter timetable

Viewed from the southbound platform, No.1450 plus its solitary auto coach pose in Tiverton station on the same day the previous shot was taken. The branch engines were housed in a small engine shed at Tiverton Junction which was a sub-shed of Exeter and they presumably only went 'home' when due for a boiler washout or other attention.
Roy Denison

There was only one intermediate station on the Tiverton branch, Halberton Halt, which was roughly half way between the two principal stations. The line, as previously mentioned, was built for double track so there was plenty of space beneath the bridge to accommodate the small halt seen here on 18th July 1964. This also had the additional benefit of providing travellers with more than adequate protection from the elements.
Roy Denison

The delightful Exe Valley line ran between Stoke Canon, on the main Exeter to Taunton line, and Morebath Junction on the cross-country Barnstaple to Taunton route, but trains usually ran through to Dulverton, just over the county border in Somerset. The branch, which was built to the standard gauge, was promoted by two entirely separate companies. The Exe Valley Railway Company obtained an Act on 30th June 1874 to construct the section from Stoke Canon to Tiverton but in the following year handed its powers to the Bristol & Exeter Railway. The line was subsequently built by the GWR and, after a considerable delay, opened on 1st May 1885. Construction of the section north of Tiverton was proposed by the Tiverton & North Devon Railway who obtained an Act in 1875 and its section became the first to carry traffic, opening on 1st August 1884. The branch was single track throughout but crossing loops were provided at Thorverton, Tiverton and Bampton. It should be pointed out that Exe Valley trains were unable to serve Stoke Canon until a new junction station was built there in 1894. In GWR days various new halts were constructed to serve scattered communities and while this was commercially desirable the additional stops added to the overall journey time which was generally 70min. for the sedate 24¾ miles-long run from Exeter to Dulverton. In the 1953–54 timetable seven trains were advertised in each direction on weekdays while a truncated Sunday service ran between Exeter and Tiverton and vice versa during the summer months. The entire line was closed completely from 7th October 1963 except for a short stub between Stoke Canon and Thorverton. For the first 3½ miles northwards from Exeter, Exe valley workings ran along the main line and had to be slotted in among fast expresses, and this must have required some ingenuity, particularly on summer Saturdays when traffic was at its height. Here, Collett-designed 1400 Class 0-4-2T No.1471 races along the main line tracks at Cowley Bridge Junction with a northbound Exe valley train on 5th July 1961. *R.C. Riley*

Table 87	EXETER, TIVERTON and DULVERTON
	(Second class only except where otherwise shewn)

Western Region 1961 summer timetable (continued opposite)

Thorverton, seen here on 3rd July 1963, was the first station north of Exeter with a passing loop and therefore possessed a signal box which is clearly visible in this shot. The main station building, located on the southbound platform, had twin gables and decorative barge boards while the opposite platform was equipped with only a waiting shelter. When the line was closed the section between Stoke Canon and Thorverton remained open for grain traffic to the local mill until 30th November 1966. *R.C. Riley*

A further, more distant view of Thorverton station taken on 15th June 1963, a rather dull and misty day. The 1.45pm Tiverton to Exeter St David's train, formed of two auto coaches propelled by a 1400 Class 0-4-2T, stands in the down platform. The line to the mill diverged sharply to the right and is not visible in this picture. The mill, which was linked to the 'main line' by a short siding in about 1898, used to produce considerable railborne traffic. Note the goods shed and yard in the foreground; the yard seems to be reasonably busy which is, perhaps, surprising bearing in mind that the branch was closed only four months after this picture was taken. *Gerald Daniels*

		WEEK DAYS																		SUNDAYS				
Miles		am	am	am	am	am	pm	pm	pm	pm	pm	pm	pm	pm	pm	pm	pm	pm	am	am	pm	pm	pm	pm
			E	S	S		S		E	S	E	E			E		W	E		S	H	H	H	H
—	Dulverton .. .. dep	7 15	8 10	9 27	9 45	11 30		1 5	1 03	2 53	4 2		..	5 30		7 10		..	9 30		Z			
1¾	Morebath Junction Halt ..	7 19	8 14	9 32	9 49	11 34		1 9	1 43	2 93	4 6		..	5 34		7 14		..	9 34					
3¾	Bampton (Devon) ..	7 29	8 19	9 37	9 54	11 39		1 14	1 93	3 43	5 1		5 39	6 07	7 19		..	9 98					
5¾	Cove Halt ..	7 34	8 24	9 42	9 59	11 44		1 19	2 43	3 93	5 6		..	6 44		7 24		..	9 43					
8½	Bolham Halt	7 42	8 32	9 50	10 7	11 52		1 27	3 23	4 74	4 ..		5 52		7 32		..	9 50					
10½	Tiverton .... { arr	7 48	8 38	9 56	10 13	11 57		1 33	3 83	5 34	4 10		5 57	6 15	7 38		..	9 55					
	dep	7 50	8 40	10 0	10 16			1 36	4 24	0 4	1 15	2 26	0	..	7 39	8 20	9 50		10 0	9 20	11 5	4 55	7	0 8 53
11½	West Exe Halt	7 52	8 42	10 1	10 18			1 38	4 44	4	1 35	2 36	2		7 41	8 23				9 22	11 7	4 57	7	2
14½	Cadeleigh ..	8 0	8 50	10 11	10 26			1 46	5 24	1 14	2 15	3 16	16		7 49	8 31				9 30	11 15	5	57	10
15¾	Burn (for Butterleigh) Halt	8 3	..		..			1 50	5 64	1 34	4 25													
17¾	Up Exe Halt ..	8 8	..		..			1 55	2	1 14	2 14	30												
18½	Thorverton	8 16	8 59	10 22	10 35			2	2 2	4 4	2 44	3 35	4 06	2 05	..	7 58	8 40			9 39	11 24	5 1 47	19	
20½	Brampford Speke Halt	8 21	9 4	10 27	10 40			2	7 2	9 4	2 94	4 66	30		8 3	8 45				9 45	11 28	5 197	24	
24½	Exeter (St. David's) .. arr	8 32	9 15	10 42	10 56			2 21	2 20	4 40	4 55	5 66	46	..	8 14	8 56	10 35			10 40	9 55	11 40	5 30 7 35	9 40

E Except Saturdays
H Commences 2nd July
S Saturdays only
W Except Saturdays. Runs 17th July to 18th August inclusive
Z First and Second class. Through Train to Newton Abbot (Table 81)

For OTHER TRAINS between Morebath Junction Halt and Dulverton, see Table 86

The Exe Valley line was a haunt of auto trains powered by former GWR 1400 Class 0-4-2T locomotives but other motive power sometimes put in an appearance. In this illustration the 6.30am Exeter St David's to Dulverton train is depicted running into Cadeleigh in the early morning sunshine behind 4575 Class 2-6-2T No.5530 on 23rd May 1958. This station, known as 'Cadeleigh & Bickleigh' until May 1906, served a hamlet just over a mile to the west so it is unlikely to have been very busy. After closure the station was taken over by the local council as a highways depot but in 1997 the entire site was acquired by a private purchaser and the station buildings restored prior to re-opening as the Devon Railway Centre, so it probably now sees as many customers on some days as it used to see in a year. The 6.30am train from Exeter was due into Cadeleigh at 6.55am and the photographer is to be heartily congratulated on taking this shot before 7.00am! One wonders if he was camping out 'on location' or, more likely, had travelled down overnight from London and caught the first train of the day up the branch which preceded the 6.30am. Either way, full marks for dedication! *Gerald Daniels*

The tiny Bolham Halt was exactly two miles north of Tiverton station and served little more than a hamlet consisting of a few buildings and the inevitable public house; the halt was opened by the GWR in June 1928. Bolham Halt was equipped with a rudimentary shelter, a single nameboard and two oil lamps. *Gerald Daniels*

Exactly three miles down the line from Bolham Halt was Cove Halt which also served a few cottages and, in this case, a post office! This photograph was taken on 15th June 1963, looking southwards towards Tiverton. Cove Halt, which dated from 1923, appears at first sight to have been deliberately hidden away in a wooded valley and, unlike its neighbour, does not seem to have the luxury of any lighting so getting off the last train there would have been an intimidating experience. At least it had some real GWR character – a 'pagoda' type waiting shelter and nameboard in true Great Western style. What more could one ask? *Gerald Daniels*

The Exeter to Dulverton line has always been known as the 'Exe Valley line' but this description is not entirely accurate because a short section of the route near Bampton actually runs along the valley of the river Batherm, a tributary of the river Exe that rises in the hills about four miles to the north. Bampton was one of the larger settlements on the line with a crossing loop, goods shed and signal box. There used to be a siding into a quarry that diverged to the left, but the quarry ceased production in 1950. This picture, looking towards Tiverton, was taken on 11th June 1962. *Gerald Daniels*

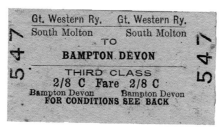

The 9.45am train from Exeter St David's to Dulverton, with 1400 Class 0-4-2T No.1468 in charge, pauses at Bampton on 11th September 1956. In the winter 1954/55 timetable eight trains were advertised on weekdays along the entire length of the line and in addition there were one or two short workings from Exeter that terminated at either Tiverton or Bampton. Journey times varied but the average time for the full trip was around 65 minutes. The 9.05pm was the last train of the day from Dulverton and this was routed to run via Tiverton Junction and took 1hr. 20min. There was great sadness when the last trains ran on 5th October 1963 and this was no doubt mixed with some anger when local people discovered that the WR operating authorities had decided to replace the final steam auto train workings with Mk.1 BR Standard coaches hauled by a Type 2 diesel, hardly an appropriate end to such a lovely branch line.
Gerald Daniels

There was a lot of wrangling between the Railway Commissioners and two local competing companies before the Exeter to Crediton line was opened as a broad gauge route on 12th May 1851. In February 1852 the North Devon Railway cut the first sod at Copplestone on an extension from Crediton towards Barnstaple and this opened on 1st August 1854. It was an easy route to work, the single track line gradually dropping down from the summit at Copplestone on moderate gradients following the twists and turns of the river Taw for most of the way. On 1st January 1863 the LSWR took over the route, which by this time had been converted to mixed gauge and, despite the LSWR being in control, a daily broad gauge goods working continued to Barnstaple until 1877, and to Crediton until 1892. The Coleford Junction (near Crediton) to Copplestone and Umberleigh to Barnstaple Junction sections were both doubled before the First World War but, apart from that, the route saw little investment and a meagre service operated due to the largely single track and difficulty of crossing full-length trains which were sometimes forced to set back with the rear in a siding. A dairy at Lapford provided heavy traffic for the railway for generations but this closed in the 1970s, while a large forest established in 1919 near Eggesford has never produced much traffic for the line. In this illustration, which was taken from a road bridge that separates the up and down platforms at Lapford, Bulleid Pacific No.34106 *Lydford* 'blows off' as it waits in the down loop for the mid-day Ilfracombe to Waterloo express, with No.34002 *Salisbury* in charge, to pass through the station. Note that on the left of the picture the station's name is displayed in whitewashed stones, probably the handiwork of an enthusiastic member of staff, while the signal box is partially visible through the smoke and steam. This photograph was taken on 3rd August 1963. *Gerald Daniels*

Another shot taken at Lapford on the same day, this time showing No.34106 *Lydford*, in charge of the 8.35am Waterloo to Ilfracombe train, pulling away from the down platform which is just discernible through the arch of the bridge. The rather unconventional layout at Lapford came about because there was no space for a second platform opposite the original single line platform (seen on the left) so it had to be built beyond the road bridge as depicted here. Rather strangely, both platforms were on the same side of the lines they served. Lapford was very busy with goods traffic at one time: note the vans in the yard on the right, a creamery having been established here in 1928. Unfortunately, as previously stated, it was closed in the 1970s. *Gerald Daniels*

Exchanging the tokens at Morchard Road. Running the railway has always required a degree of teamwork and in this picture the signalman at Morchard Road station, south of Barnstaple, is in position to exchange the tokens with the driver of the up 'Atlantic Coast Express', *en route* to London, on 27th August 1962. The locomotive is filthy Bulleid 'Battle of Britain' Pacific No.34074 *46 Squadron* which was presumably working only as far as Exeter – it would not do to have such a dirty engine on the main part of the journey of such a prestigious train. Note the lovely old signal box, platform oil lamp and concrete running-in board. *Lens of Sutton Association*

The Exeter to Barnstaple line may have been built originally as a broad gauge line but since the takeover by the LSWR it became exclusively 'Southern' in character. Barnstaple saw a mixture of both SR and GWR locomotives, however, the latter working in from Taunton, so the 'Southern' atmosphere there was a trifle diluted. In this picture former GWR 4300 Class 'Mogul' No.6363 is seen on the turntable road at Barnstaple shed on 20th July 1964 with a SR 'Mogul' stabled further down the siding. By the date of this photograph the shed building at Barnstaple, which is visible on the left, was reduced to little more than a skeleton and hardly worthy of the name 'shed'. The shed was actually a two-road building with an adjacent coal stage and there was also a 50ft turntable, adequate to turn a Maunsell 'Mogul' but too short for larger locomotives which presumably had to be turned at Ilfracombe. The ramshackle shed at Barnstaple was closed in 1964 and was no doubt razed to the ground shortly afterwards – it was probably less than an hour's work for the demolition men! *R.C. Riley*

The down 'Devon Belle' from Waterloo to Ilfracombe, with Bulleid 'West Country' Class Pacific No.34025 *Whimple* in charge, crosses the river Taw, between Barnstaple Junction and Barnstaple Town stations, on 16th June 1950. This train made its inaugural run on 20th June 1947 and the Southern Railway hoped that it would stimulate holiday travel after the grim war years. It was comprised entirely of Pullman cars and offered a very high standard of comfort and luxury; there was even an observation car on the rear which enabled passengers to admire the scenery as the train sped along. All seats could be reserved which was quite a novelty at that time. In 1950 the down working left Waterloo at 12.00pm and the up portion from Ilfracombe (there was a separate Plymouth portion) departed at the same time, the journey time being just under 5½ hours. The down 'Devon Belle's first stop was advertised as Sidmouth Junction but in reality the train stopped at Wilton South, just west of Salisbury, to change engines because the 'Southern' did not have any water troughs. Sadly, patronage was not up to expectations and 'The Devon Belle' ran for the last time at the end of the 1954 summer timetable. *J.J.Smith collection / Bluebell Railway Museum*

Another former GWR 'Mogul', No.7337, in very dirty condition, rolls into Braunton station with an unidentified 'up' train on an overcast 25th July 1964. The Act authorising the construction of the line from Barnstaple to Ilfracombe was passed on 4th July 1870 but construction was bedevilled by a dire shortage of navvies to undertake the extensive civil engineering works along the line that included many cuttings and embankments, plus an iron bridge across the river Taw; the route eventually opened for business on 20th July 1874. The Ilfracombe line had some of the steepest inclines to be found on any main line in Great Britain: three miles at 1 in 40 up to a summit at Mortehoe and then a descent to Ilfracombe on a tortuous gradient of 1 in 36. One wonders if enginemen relished tackling the 1 in 36 gradient from a standing start in Ilfracombe station – this must have been quite a challenge on a wet day. *R.C. Riley*

The motive power used on the Barnstaple to Ilfracombe line was a mixture of 'Southern' and former GWR classes and in this picture Maunsell 'Mogul' No.31834 is seen piloting an unidentified 4300 Class 'Mogul' up the 1 in 40 climb to Mortehoe station which was situated on the 600ft contour. Normally, northbound trains were banked from Braunton and the signalman at Mortehoe must have been kept really busy on a summer Saturday with trains in both directions plus one or two banking engines. It is likely that in this case both locomotives were needed at Ilfracombe, hence the use of a pilot engine in preference to a banker. *Alan Reeve*

The line between Barnstaple and Ilfracombe was in many respects like a railway version of a fairground big dipper which went up on a very steep gradient and came down, in this particular case, on an even steeper one! Certainly the descent of the 1 in 36 gradient to Ilfracombe station offered unrivalled views out to sea. Here, Bulleid 'West Country' Class Pacific No.34035 *Shaftesbury* carefully descends the incline towards Ilfracombe in August 1962 and, no doubt, the driver's hand was firmly clasping the brake valve as he came down the bank. This proved to be *Shaftesbury*'s final full year in traffic because it was one of the four Bulleid Pacifics withdrawn in June 1963 – the first inroads into the 'West Country' and 'Battle of Britain' classes. *Alan Reeve*

The final steam train from Ilfracombe ran on 3rd October 1965, this being the Southern Counties Touring Society 'Exeter Flyer' rail tour from London. The tour was split at Barnstaple, one portion running to Torrington while another ran to Ilfracombe, hence the short formation. This train really lived up to its title and both the up and down journeys between Waterloo and Exeter were completed in an extremely fast time, well up to the standard of the legendary 'Atlantic Coast Express'; motive power was Bulleid 'Merchant Navy' Pacific No.35022 *Holland-America Line*. The tour was over-subscribed and the train seen here is a repeat run to cater for the demand using the same engines. Here BR Standard Class 4MT 2-6-4T No.80043 is seen awaiting departure from the Devon resort on that date. The station at Ilfracombe may appear to be almost up in the clouds and indeed it was perched 200ft above the Bristol Channel, and it is likely that its location high above the town did little to foster local traffic. Passenger services ceased between Barnstaple Junction and Ilfracombe from 5th October 1970 and, despite local preservation attempts, the tracks were subsequently lifted thus thwarting any resumption of the service under private auspices along one of the most spectacular lines in Great Britain.
Alan Reeve

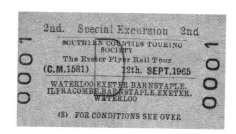

The Padstow portion of the 'up' 'Atlantic Coast Express' has just passed Cowley Bridge Junction, about two miles north of Exeter St David's, behind Bulleid 'West Country' Pacific No.34011 *Tavistock*; this picture was taken on 5th July 1961. Part of Cowley Bridge Junction signal box can just be discerned beyond the road overbridge. The river Exe is just out of the picture on the left. *R.C. Riley*

EXETER TO LAUNCESTON

North Tawton station, between Crediton and Okehampton, is seen in this illustration with Bulleid Pacific No.34078 *222 Squadron* standing at the down platform at the head of (what appears to be) the westbound 'Atlantic Coast Express' on 25th July 1964. Passengers arriving at North Tawton were left in no doubt about the name of the station: note the huge sign on the front of the signal box. Railway history in this area is complicated due to the proliferation of various small, local companies before they were amalgamated with the mighty LSWR. The section between Crediton and Coleford Junction (where the Barnstaple line diverges from the Okehampton route) was built by the North Devon Railway and opened on 1st August 1854. The Coleford Junction to North Tawton stretch was, however, promoted by the Devon & Cornwall Railway and was brought into use on 1st November 1865. North Tawton remained the terminus for a number of years because progress on the extension to Okehampton was slow due to shortage of funds. The line was eventually opened to Okehampton on 3rd October 1871 and the Devon & Cornwall Railway survived only another year, before being absorbed by the LSWR. *R.C. Riley*

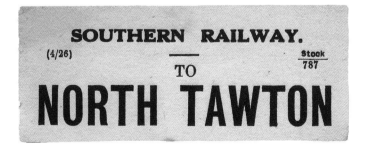

SOUTHERN RAILWAY.

(4/26)
Stock
787
TO
NORTH TAWTON

A real thoroughbred, former LSWR T9 Class 4-4-0 No.30717, poses for its picture on the turntable at Okehampton shed on 14th July 1959. A turntable for visiting engines had been provided at Okehampton almost from the outset but there was no shed until a wooden structure was built in the mid-1890s. Wood proved to be vulnerable to fire, however, the entire shed being totally destroyed by a conflagration in 1920. A replacement was built using concrete blocks with an asbestos roof and this edifice, which reputedly cost £1,500, is just visible on the right of the photograph. The shed was single ended, had a 50ft diameter turntable and a small coaling stage. In order to accommodate larger locomotives a 70ft diameter turntable was installed in 1947 and this enabled S15 Class engines, which powered many stone trains to and from Meldon quarry, to be turned without the need to uncouple the tender. The depot, always a sub-shed of Exmouth Junction, lasted until 1966 when it was demolished. *R.C. Riley*

British Transport Commission (S)

OKEHAMPTON

(S.2) PLATFORM TICKET 2d

Available one hour on day of issue only.
Not valid in trains. Not transferable.
To be given up when leaving platform.

For conditions see over

Meldon viaduct is probably one of the best-known railway structures in the south of England and offered spectacular views to travellers, with Dartmoor and a sweeping vista towards Yes Tor (2,028 feet above sea level) on the south side and, to the north, the rolling hills of north Devon. The viaduct was constructed in the early 1870s and first came into regular use on 12th October 1874 when the LSWR's single track Okehampton to Lydford line opened for traffic. The viaduct was of a rather spindly apppearance with six girder spans supported by metal lattice piers and is situated on a 30 chains curve; at its highest point it is 150ft above the floor of a ravine through which the West Okement river flows. In 1879 the line was doubled and a second viaduct, with its piers intertwined with the first, was built at the same time. Following closure of the line on 6th May 1968 the former 'up' line remained *in situ* as a headshunt for the quarry whilst in the early 1970s steel decking was laid on the space formerly occupied by the down line for use by lorries taking stone from Meldon quarry to the site of a new reservoir. In this illustration Maunsell 'Mogul' No.31853 is depicted crossing the structure with a lightweight, westbound train formed of two coaches and a van in July 1963. *R.C. Riley*

A blot on the landscape? A gaping hole in the hillside and huge waste tips immediately identify the site of Meldon quarry which dominates the background of this shot of Bulleid 'West Country' Pacific No.34029 *Lundy* crossing Meldon viaduct with a Padstow train in 1957. Meldon quarry dated from 1897 and was notable for producing a particularly hard and durable type of rock that was ideal for use as track ballast. In the past the quarry used to provide massive quantities of stone for the Southern Region and regular trains ran to Eastleigh, Hoo Junction (near Gravesend), Woking and Tonbridge. Note the quarrymen's cottages in the middle of the picture. The line steepens to 1 in 58 just beyond this point and the sand drag, in the foreground on the right, and its associated catch points were strategically positioned to prevent runaway vehicles from causing too much havoc. *Colin Hogg*

It is often said that many boys dreamed of being an engine driver when they grew up and, no doubt, quite a few realised their ambition. It was, however, a dirty and laborious occupation involving working at all times of the day and night and many people who aspired to be drivers probably finished up in other walks of life. The next best thing for a steam aficionado, therefore, was a footplate ride for which, very occasionally, official permission would be forthcoming but the vast majority of footplate trips were probably given with only the 'official' permission of the crew when the local motive power inspector was not looking! The late Dick Riley had many friends on the railways and on 15th July 1960 he was lucky enough to have a footplate ride on T9 Class 4-4-0 No.30719, working the 9.56am Okehampton to Padstow, over the North Cornwall line and this shot was taken at Meldon Junction where the Plymouth line, on the left, diverged from the route to Halwill Junction and Launceston. What a wonderful experience, riding with the crew on a real old timer, a locomotive that first saw the light of day way back in 1899 when it emerged from the works of Dubs & Co. in Glasgow. The North Cornwall line, which ran from Halwill Junction to Wadebridge via Launceston, was one of the most scenic byways in the south of England and the lovely countryside no doubt added to Dick Riley's enjoyment. Great! *R.C. Riley*

A view of Tower Hill station (218¾ miles from Waterloo) showing No.30719 waiting in the down platform for the up 'Atlantic Coast Express' to appear – the trains were booked to cross there. The station nestled in the deep valley of the river Carey and, with the exception of a row of railway cottages, there was no habitation in the immediate vicinity. The train comprised just two coaches and a van and this gives some indication of the totally unremunerative nature of this rural line. Many of the stations on this line were converted into comfortable homes following closure, but the buildings at Tower Hill were demolished and today only a few fragments of the former station remain. This shot was also taken on 15th July 1960. Note that the unfortunate guard has been relegated to travelling in the van, this being the only brake van on the train. The history of the section of line between Halwill Junction and Launceston can be traced back to 18th August 1882 when the North Cornwall Railway obtained an Act to construct a line from Halwill Junction to Launceston and Padstow. The Halwill to Launceston stretch opened on 21st July 1886 while the route onwards to Padstow, which is entirely in Cornwall and therefore outside the scope of this book, eventually opened throughout on 27th March 1899 after numerous delays due to shortage of funds and the route's difficult terrain. *R.C. Riley*

When the LSWR's route to Exeter was completed in 1860 a terminus was sited in the city centre abutting Queen Street on its western side and it was originally known as 'Exeter Queen Street' station. The station used to have an overall roof which made the platforms very gloomy but the entire station was rebuilt in the early 1930s and officially opened on 1st July 1933; its name was changed to 'Exeter Central' from that date. In this illustration, which dates from 17th May 1964, the very pleasing frontage of the station is seen; note the attractive stonework and cupola. Regrettably, some of the destinations served by the 'through expresses' no longer have direct trains from Exeter Central while some areas have completely lost their rail services. *Stuart Ackley collection*

Low evening sunshine just peeping through the clouds, a nice selection of old GWR signals, the flood plain of the river Exe and a nearby hill all combine to produce a sparkling image of Maunsell 'Mogul' No.31830 hauling a two-coach local train at the approach to Cowley Bridge Junction in 1957. The precise identity of the train is unknown but it is believed to be a local working from Exeter Central to Plymouth Friary. The engine was 'blowing off' as the train approached the photographer and the escaping white steam really adds life to the shot. *Colin Hogg*

A train from Plymouth to London, hauled by Bulleid 'West Country' Pacific No.34023 *Blackmore Vale*, leaves 'Southern' metals at Cowley Bridge Junction and joins former GWR tracks for the run into Exeter St David's station. The short, four coach formation will be noted but more carriages would have been attached, probably including a restaurant car, at Exeter Central. This shot was taken on 16th July 1958. The lines diverging to the right lead to Tiverton Junction and Taunton and the waters of the river Exe are just visible on the left. The yellow board just beyond the signal box warns train crews that there is a temporary speed restriction just ahead while the number '20' indicates the maximum speed permitted (20mph) on the affected section of line. The stretch of line from Exeter to Crediton was originally broad gauge and opened on 12th May 1851. *R.C. Riley*

The line between Exeter and Okehampton saw a constant stream of trains to and from Meldon Quarry and it would be amiss to produce a book about the closing years of steam in Devon without including at least one shot of such a working. This view, which was photographed on 28th August 1962, shows a loaded train of ballast hoppers from Meldon heading eastwards at Crediton with BR Standard Class 4MT 2-6-4T No.80064 in charge. Originally Crediton was the terminus of a broad gauge branch from Exeter but the station seen here is actually the second one to be erected in the town and dates from 1854 when the broad gauge line to Barnstaple was opened. The station became mixed gauge in 1863 and in 1876 through trains to Plymouth via Lydford started running, so Crediton really was on the railway map in a big way. Broad gauge goods trains continued to operate until 1892 and the GWR retained a presence until 1903. Crediton station was on the fringe of the town and passengers were gradually lost to the roads, but goods traffic held up quite well. When the area west of Salisbury fell into the hands of the WR in 1963 the writing was on the wall and services were quickly reduced in scope, the first victim being the Bude and North Cornwall line trains while the Plymouth trains were cut back to Okehampton in May 1968 and withdrawn entirely in 1972. The main goods yard is on the left in this picture, but originally there were goods facilities on both sides of the line; all goods traffic was discontinued in December 1967. Note the gas lighting and old 'Southern' signs on the lamp posts. *Lens of Sutton Association*

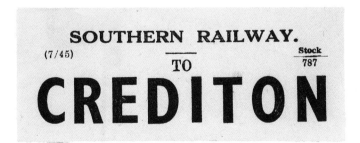

Okehampton station, which lost its passenger services from 5th June 1972, is pictured at some time in the 1950s when it was still possible to catch a through train to Waterloo; this view is looking westwards. The principal station buildings, rebuilt in brick in the 1930s, were located on the up side while a footbridge of lattice construction gave access to the down platform from where trains ran to Plymouth and north Cornwall. *Stuart Ackley collection*

The 1950s were hardly the heyday of Okehampton station but in this portrait, taken on 13th July 1957, it does seem to be quite busy with a fair number of passengers waiting on the platforms. It appears to have been a really nice day with large puffy clouds scudding across the sky. This view, looking eastwards towards Exeter, reveals a train without an engine in the down platform, probably the rear portion of a through express from London. Perhaps the gentleman walking along the track was the station shunter who was waiting to couple up a locomotive that had not yet appeared. Regrettably, the network of lightly trafficked routes that fanned out from Okehampton, to Bude, Exeter, north Cornwall and Plymouth, was soon to be removed from the railway map in a series of savage cuts that deprived many rural communities of their rail connection and many people questioned the motives of the Western Region who seemed determined to close as many former 'Southern' routes as possible. *Lens of Sutton Association*

The first railway to reach Lydford was the broad gauge branch from Plymouth to Launceston via Tavistock which was opened on 1st June 1865. The LSWR extended their line from Okehampton and its trains were able to reach Plymouth using the existing broad gauge line which was converted to mixed gauge. In 1890 the Plymouth, Devonport & South Western Junction Railway brought into use its line from Devonport to Lydford and this gave the LSWR an independent route to Plymouth. The trains, worked by the LSWR from the outset, terminated at North Road initially but were extended to Friary station in 1891. This picture was taken on 23rd June 1962 looking southwards with the church on Brent Tor prominent on the horizon. The former 'Southern' tracks are in the middle of the shot while on the right a two-coach WR train from Plymouth to Launceston, hauled by a 4575 Class 2-6-2T, slows for its Lydford station stop. The wartime link between the two routes is clearly visible but the rusty rail surfaces indicate it had not seen recent use. The sidings beyond the link were laid for housing government stores during World War Two in preference to storage in the Plymouth area which was more susceptible to bombing. Lydford constitutes one of the worst examples of senseless duplication of railway facilities – surely one route into Plymouth would have stood a better chance of long-term survival? *J.J.Smith collection / Bluebell Railway Museum*

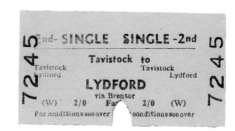

Brentor station appears to be deserted while a Plymouth to Launceston train scuttles by on the adjacent former GWR branch. Once again, Brent Tor church forms a distinctive backdrop. The station's principal building, which incorporated the station house, was on the down side with a stone-built platform shelter opposite and the former GWR line immediately behind as seen in the picture. The latter did not serve the village of Brentor, choosing instead to stop at Mary Tavy & Blackdown station further down the valley of the river Burn, a tributary of the river Tavy. Interestingly, the bridge over the 'Southern' line from where the picture was taken was a substantial stone-built structure, whereas that across the former GWR single line was a steel span. One wonders how many passengers waiting at Brentor have collected their belongings on hearing a train approaching only to find it was on the old GWR line and would not be stopping to pick them up! This picture was taken on 23rd June 1962.
J.J. Smith collection / Bluebell Railway Museum

Brentor station was situated on a short level stretch of track but there was a mile-long 1 in 75 climb until Lydford station, also on a level section, was reached. After leaving Lydford trains faced a further 6½ miles of climbing until they reached the summit in a cutting at Sourton Down. Bulleid Pacifics were extremely powerful machines, however, and the gradients on this route are unlikely to have taxed No.34109 *Sir Trafford Leigh-Mallory,* hauling a modest eight-coach load, which is seen here passing Brentor with the 11.10am Plymouth to Waterloo train also on 23rd June 1962. Note the station building's delightful stonework and graceful 'barley sugar' oil lamp.
J.J.Smith collection / Bluebell Railway Museum

The frontage of Tavistock (North) station, seen here on 17th July 1962, was really eye-catching with its delightful higgledy-piggledy stonework, tall chimneys and dormer windows, not to mention the bay window at the front of the station house. Built by the Plymouth, Devonport & South Western Junction Railway the station was a relative latecomer on the scene for a main-line station, not opening until 2nd June 1890 when the Lydford to Devonport route came into use. It was, apparently, the only one of that company's stations to be favoured with platform canopies. The line down from Lydford required substantial earthworks, plus viaducts and tunnels, and construction of Tavistock station also provided the navvies with a tough job, the station site being blasted out of a steep hillside. The weekday service from Tavistock in the early 1960s included five expresses to Waterloo and a through train to Brighton via Salisbury, plus a few local services from Plymouth that ran as far as Tavistock or Brentor. This pattern lasted until September 1966 when the London trains were withdrawn, while the Brighton service survived until the following March. It should be noted that the suffix 'North' was added by BR after nationalisation in order to distinguish the two Tavistock stations. Goods facilities were withdrawn in February 1966 while passenger trains, such as they were, continued until 6th May 1968. *Stuart Ackley collection*

The cream paintwork, grey station stonework and bright red telephone box all combine to make a reasonably colourful photograph of Bere Alston station which is depicted in this portrait dated 28th August 1961. This shot was taken from the footbridge at the western end of the station and shows a Plymouth-bound passenger train with Bulleid Pacific No.34056 *Croydon* in charge. Bere Alston was the junction for the branch for Callington which opened in 1908. Note the signal box, which presumably controlled all train movements at the station, towards the far end of the up platform. *R.C. Riley*

SOUTHERN RAILWAY.

(12/34)   Stock

BRIGHTON TO   787

BERE ALSTON

British Transport Commission (S)

BERE ALSTON

PLATFORM TICKET 2d.

Available one hour on day of issue only.
Not valid in trains. Not transferable.
To be given up when leaving platform.

For conditions see over

8252

EXETER TO PLYMOUTH VIA OKEHAMPTON

The substantial goods shed at Devonport King's Road station dominates this picture which was taken on 30th April 1961; the branch to Stonehouse Pool and the former LSWR's ocean liner terminal passed underneath the goods yard and shed in a short tunnel, the mouth of which can be seen on the left. The station here was formerly called 'Devonport & Stonehouse' and opened on 18th May 1876 when the LSWR entered Plymouth over the GWR mixed gauge line from Lydford via Tavistock. It was a grand terminus located in a part of the city which, at that time, buzzed with commercial activity due to its close proximity to the dockyard. It remained a terminus until the Plymouth, Devonport & South Western Junction Railway's line from Lydford via Bere Alston was opened in 1890, the station becoming a through one, and the designation of the up and down lines was immediately reversed. Ominously, Devonport station looks deserted in this picture and closed to passengers on 7th September 1964, when SR traffic was diverted via the former GWR route using a wartime connection at St Budeaux. *R.C. Riley*

Plymouth Friary – the city's forgotten station. This Plymouth terminus was opened by the LSWR on 1st July 1891 but the station was destined to have a relatively short existence. Trains on the 'Southern' route from Waterloo used former GWR tracks through Plymouth (North Road) station to reach Lipson Junction, and then Mount Gould Junction, before running alongside the river Plym to Friary Junction where they gained their own tracks. From there the line swung almost due west, having turned through 180 degrees since leaving North Road, and then ran up a short, but steep gradient before Friary station was reached. The station consisted of two main platforms with two shorter bay platforms which could only

accommodate three- or four-coach trains. In this picture, which was the only shot of this station submitted for use in this book, former GWR 'Mogul' No.7333 is seen awaiting departure with the 2.35pm working to Exeter via Okehampton on 20th August 1958; this was presumably a service operated by WR crews and locomotives for route familiarisation. Less than a month after this picture was taken Friary station was closed to passengers and converted into a goods depot but the station buildings were demolished in the mid-1970s and the site is now occupied by a new road and housing. *Edwin Wilmshurst*

The line from Barnstaple to Bideford was originally broad gauge, the first section as far as Fremington being opened in August 1854 by the North Devon Railway, but it should be noted that horse-drawn goods traffic had been conveyed between Barnstaple and Fremington since August 1848. On 2nd November 1855 the line was extended to Bideford by the Bideford Extension Railway but within a few years the LSWR absorbed all of the local companies operating in the area and the broad gauge tracks were converted to mixed gauge, thus enabling standard gauge trains to serve Bideford from 1st March 1863. There were two intermediate stations between Barnstaple and Bideford, Fremington and Instow, and the last-mentioned station is depicted in this photograph which was taken on 9th June 1962, looking towards Bideford. *Gerald Daniels*

An M7 Class engine on the 'ACE'! The multi-portioned 'Atlantic Coast Express' was famous for its fast schedule between London and Exeter but once it had reached Exeter some portions of the train were routed along secondary lines and slowed down considerably. One of the train's portions served Torrington and was uncoupled from the Ilfracombe section at Barnstaple Junction. In this illustration the Torrington part of the train is seen at Bideford behind M7 Class 0-4-4T No.30255 on 12th September 1959, the M7 probably being more than adequate motive power for this final stretch of the journey for which the load was only four coaches and a van. Even so, the idea of an M7 on the 'ACE' does sound a bit unlikely. *John Langford*

BARNSTAPLE TO TORRINGTON

A strategically positioned road bridge at Torrington gave railway photographers a splendid view of comings and goings, such as they were, at this quiet country station. The train standing in the platform is from Barnstaple and has arrived behind Ivatt-designed Class 2MT 2-6-2T No.41310. In 1865 the LSWR was authorised to build a standard gauge line from Bideford to Torrington and this became operational in July 1872. The Torrington to Halwill Junction line was authorised in 1914 under a Light Railway Order and built by Col. H.F. Stephens, the prodigious light railway builder. It was the last line to be built by him and also the final railway route of any consequence to be constructed in the west of England. Part of the line followed the route of the Torrington and Marland Railway's 3ft gauge tramway built in the 1880s. The first sod was cut for the new line on 30th June 1922 and it opened on 27th July 1925. The principal reason for the line's construction was to service the mineral and clay workings at Marland and Meeth. Milk traffic was also a major source of revenue at Torrington for many years: note the tank wagons on the right of the picture. Like many principal stations in north Devon, Torrington was not conveniently situated in relation to the town it served, being a mile away from the town centre which was 200ft above the station. This photograph was taken on 24th September 1962. *R.C. Riley*

The line southwards from Torrington to Halwill Junction was a true backwater with only two slow, through trains on weekdays only, plus a few short workings, and is unlikely to have attracted many *bona fide* customers. The painfully slow trains, ungated road crossings, lovely scenery and, of course, guaranteed steam haulage made it a firm favourite, however, among those railway enthusiasts lucky enough to witness its eccentricities. In this absolute gem of a picture a mixed train hauled by Ivatt 2-6-2T No.41238 crosses the river Torridge south of Torrington in superb evening light on 24th September 1962. The identity of the train is unknown but it is believed to be one of the short workings, the 4.37pm from Petrockstow which was due in Torrington at 5.14pm. *R.C. Riley*

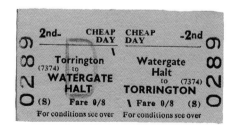

On 27th March 1965 the Railway Correspondence & Travel Society and Plymouth Railway Circle jointly sponsored the 'Exmoor Ranger' rail tour which started in Exeter and covered the line from Barnstaple to Ilfracombe and also that from Barnstaple to Taunton. The train naturally travelled to Barnstaple using the most interesting and little-known route and is depicted here approaching the viaduct across the river Torridge just outside Torrington. The locomotives used on this section of the tour were Ivatt 2-6-2Ts Nos.41206 and 41291 which are seen here coupled bunker to bunker hauling a multi-coloured five coach train. Passenger services had been withdrawn from the Halwill Junction to Torrington section from 1st March 1965 and the section of track between Halwill and Meeth Halt, which was to be closed completely, was reportedly kept intact for some weeks after the closure to enable this train to operate. The stretch from Meeth to Torrington was retained for goods traffic. Could the organisers have chosen a more obscure route? *Roy Hobbs*

Table 43 **HALWILL, HATHERLEIGH and TORRINGTON**

Miles	Week Days only	am	am SX		am SO		pm SX	pm	
	Halwill .. .. .. dep	..	**1038**	..	**1052**	..	..	6 30	..
3	Hole	....	1047	....	11 1	....	....	6 39	....
7¾	Hatherleigh	..	11 5	..	1119	..	..	6 57	..
10	Meeth Halt	....	1116	....	1132	....	....	7 8	....
12¾	Petrockstow	7 55	1128	..	1142	..	4 37	7 18	..
14¾	Dunsbear Halt	8 4	1140	....	1152	....	4 46	7 28	....
16	Yarde Halt	8 10	1145	..	1157	..	4 52	7 34	..
18¾	Watergate Halt	8 24	1159	....	1211	....	5 6	7 48	....
20½	**Torrington** .. .. arr	**8 32**	**12 6**	..	**1218**	..	**5 14**	**7 56**	..

Miles	Week Days only	am	am		pm SX		pm SO	
	Torrington .. .. dep	**6 25**	**8 52**	..	**4 0**	..	**4 40**	..
1¾	Watergate Halt	6 32	8 59	....	4 7	....	4 47	....
4½	Yarde Halt	6 46	9 13	..	4 20	..	5 1	..
5½	Dunsbear Halt	6†52	9 18	....	4 25	....	5 6	....
7¾	Petrockstow	..	9 28	..	4 34	..	5 16	..
10½	Meeth Halt	....	9 38	....	4 44	....	5 26	....
12¾	Hatherleigh	..	9 48	..	4 54	..	5 36	..
17½	Hole	....	10 8	....	5 13	....	5 56	....
20½	**Halwill** .. .. .. arr	..	**1018**	..	**5 23**	..	**6 6**	..

SO Saturdays only **SX** Mondays to Fridays † Arrival

Southern Region 1957 summer timetable

(7496)
2nd - SPECIAL ARRANGEMENT
0090
Railways Correspondence & Travel Society
Plymouth Railway Circle
"The Exmoor Ranger" 27th MARCH, '65
Exeter (St. Davids), Okehampton N.D. & C.J.L. Rly., Barnstaple (Victoria Road), Ilfracombe, Barnstaple Junct., Dulverton, Taunton, Exeter (St. Davids)
(W) For conditions see over
0090

Petrockstow was a charming little station with an attractive stone-built main building with a small canopy, oil lamps and neat running-in board. There were also two goods sidings, but goods facilities were withdrawn from 7th September 1964. The Torrington to Halwill Junction line was, of course, built 'on the cheap' as a light railway and consequently there were un-gated road crossings and no signal boxes, all signalling functions being controlled from ground frames. Here, the guard and driver discuss the likelihood of a passenger appearing – unfortunately the station was remote from the village – while Ivatt 2-6-2T Class 2MT No.41312 simmers at the platform on 25th September 1962. *R.C. Riley*

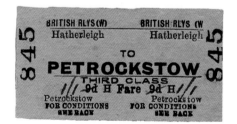

A comprehensive view of Halwill Junction station taken on a rather gloomy 28th August 1962. The footpath in the foreground leads to the platform from where Torrington trains started, while prominent on the left is the signal box which seems to tower above the entire station. A bunker-first Ivatt 2-6-2T stands beside the main station building while the goods yard is on the right of the shot. Perhaps the main source of interest in this photograph is the gentleman standing on top of the signal. The signal lamps had to be attended to regularly for obvious safety reasons and lampmen were employed to ensure the burners were topped up with paraffin and the wicks were in good condition. It was a typical 'day in, day out' job for the staff involved that was nowhere near the high profile accorded to an engine driver but was, nonetheless, vital to the safe operation of the railway. *Lens of Sutton Association*

A porter drags a trolley carrying a single package along the platform at Halwill Junction on 20th July 1962 – it must have been a particularly heavy parcel! The Devon & Cornwall Railway, a subsidiary of the LSWR, obtained an Act on 7th July 1873 for a line from Meldon Junction to Holsworthy and the first trains ran on 20th January 1879. In 1895 the LSWR obtained parliamentary authority to extend the line to Bude and this opened on 10th August 1898. Initially the station here was known as 'Halwill & Beaworthy' but it was later re-named 'Halwill for Beaworthy' and, to add to the confusion, the signal box bore the name 'Halwill Junction'. The original 1879 station buildings, on the left of the shot, were still extant in 1962, and largely unaltered apart from the chimneys. The pair of bracket signals at the end of the platform will be noted; one served the main line platform while the other, on the left, controlled movements from the bay. The higher signals referred to train movements on the North Cornwall line while the lower signals were for the Bude branch. *Stuart Ackley collection*

The 'Exmoor Ranger' rail tour, *en route* to Barnstaple with a pair of Ivatt Class 2MT locomotives in charge, rolls into Halwill Junction station on 27th March 1965. Like a number of small country junction stations, Halwill was situated almost in the middle of nowhere, apart from the village and a cluster of buildings that sprung up after the arrival of the railway. Halwill Junction was normally very quiet but suddenly came to life when trains arrived almost simultaneously from various directions. These bursts of activity were followed by another period of slumber. This panoramic shot appears to have been taken from the steps of the lofty signal box which had a very commanding view of operations. *Roy Hobbs*

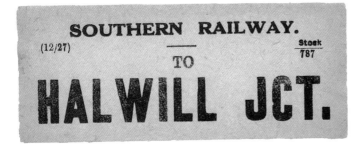

Exeter St Thomas station was opened by the SDR on 30th May 1846 and had a wooden train shed, and at first only a single platform. The station building housed the company's offices and had an imposing, attractive frontage. When the line from Exeter to Dawlish was doubled in 1861 the opportunity was taken to enlarge the station which was very busy owing to it being much closer to the city centre than the somewhat remote St David's station. The glass was removed from the overall roof in the 1950s and, sadly, the skeleton of the roof was dismantled in 1971. This picture was taken, looking northwards, on 4th March 1961; note the gas lighting. *John Langford*

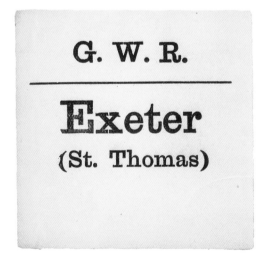

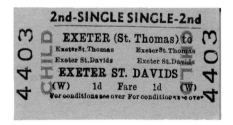

The section of line from Exeter to Newton Abbot was opened in stages by the South Devon Railway (SDR) and initially used Brunel's ill-fated atmospheric system. The SDR was taken over by the GWR in 1878. The 15 miles-long stretch as far as Teignmouth was opened to passengers on 30th May 1846 while passenger services to Newton Abbot commenced on 30th December 1846. In this illustration 2884 Class Collett-designed 2-8-0 No.3840 is depicted passing through Dawlish Warren station with a westbound goods working on 3rd July 1957. These locomotives were very powerful and the short string of wagons forming its train is unlikely to have taxed No.3840 unduly. In 1905 a rail motor service was introduced to augment trains between Exeter and Teignmouth and a new halt, called Warren Platform, was brought into use during the same year. Warren Platform was re-named Dawlish Warren from 1st October 1911 but did not survive much longer because it was replaced by a new station of the same name from 23rd September 1912. *R.C. Riley*

In the period covered by this book there were two routes between Exeter and Plymouth, the former GWR line via Newton Abbot and the former SR route via Okehampton. Passengers at Exeter St David's travelling to Plymouth must have found this confusing because Plymouth trains could leave the station in either a northerly or southerly direction and, indeed, services to London were the same. In order to ensure that enginemen were acquainted with both lines to Plymouth route familiarisation workings were an everyday occurrence and in this picture a beautifully prepared Bulleid 'Battle of Britain' Pacific No.34060 *25 Squadron* is seen rounding the curve at Langstone Rock between Dawlish Warren and Dawlish on 3rd July 1957. Unfortunately, the working is unidentified but judging by the non-gangwayed compartment stock forming the train it was an Exeter to Plymouth 'local', probably the 11.35am Exeter St David's to Plymouth North Road that ran on Mondays to Fridays only. *R.C. Riley*

Undoubtedly the finest locomotives that could be observed between Dawlish and Teignmouth during the closing years of the steam era were the mighty 'King' Class 4-6-0s that first saw the light of day back in 1927. These magnificent locomotives, as previously mentioned, were at the time of their introduction the most powerful express passenger engines in Great Britain. In this picture the 6.25am Penzance to Paddington train, hauled by No.6029 *King Edward VIII*, is seen apparently coasting along at Sprey Point east of Teignmouth on 1st July 1957. The cliffs adjacent to the line, stretch of blue sea on the left and rolling Devon countryside in the background provide the perfect setting. The chalked number on the engine's smokebox is the train identification number which was displayed to assist signalmen and station staff; in the case of this train the relevant instructions stated that the number was to be carried from Plymouth (North Road) to Paddington. *R.C. Riley*

Naturally, most of the WR's prestigious express trains were booked to be hauled by a 'King' Class locomotive when their very restricted route availability permitted its use. This shot depicts the up 'Mayflower' passing beneath the distinctive skew bridge at the east end of Teignmouth station. This train, as its name suggests, started at Plymouth and ran to London Paddington. The locomotive in charge is No.6026 *King John* and this photograph was taken on 14th July 1958. *R.C. Riley*

Another shot taken at the same location, this time showing much less glamorous motive power in the shape of an unidentified 4300 Class 2-6-0 hauling (what appears to be) a local train formed of pre-nationalisation GWR coaches. These 'Moguls' comprised a large class that was built over a long period, from 1911 to 1932. Most of the locomotives that formed this class were, naturally enough, built at Swindon but a batch was also constructed by Robert Stephenson & Co. This picture was taken on 1st July 1957. *R.C. Riley*

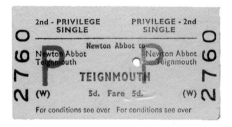

Dwarfed by the huge signal box in the background, 5101 Class 2-6-2T No.4150 brings a train of locomotive coal into Newton Abbot on 15th July 1959. Built at Swindon works and out-shopped in June 1947, No.4150 lasted in traffic until June 1965 and was subsequently preserved. *R.C. Riley*

Engine cleaning was an unglamorous, dirty and laborious task but for many footplate crews it was at least the first rung on the ladder and many top link drivers doubtless started their railway careers as cleaners. One wonders what became of the young man cleaning the locomotive's nameplate – perhaps he finished his career driving the 'Cornish Riviera Express', who knows? This portrait of No.4099 *Kilgerran Castle* was taken at Newton Abbot shed. The date of the picture is not known but it is believed it was taken in the early 1950s when No.4099 was based at the shed. The locomotive standing behind *Kilgerran Castle* is a WD Class 2-8-0 of which at least two examples were allocated to Newton Abbot in 1953.
John Ashman F.R.P.S.

BRITISH TRANSPORT COMMISSION
BRITISH RAILWAYS   BR 21716/587

NEWTON ABBOT

Dainton bank posed a formidable challenge to enginemen working heavy trains, but the sight and sound of steam locomotives working to their limit acted as a magnet for railway photographers and Dainton bank was probably one of the most photographed locations on the system. The following four pictures were all taken on the bank in the 1950s. In this really vintage shot from the early BR days 'Saint' Class 4-6-0 No.2950 *Taplow Court* assists an unidentified 'Castle' Class 4-6-0 up Dainton bank with a westbound train on 16th September 1950; the train is approaching Stoneycombe quarry where the gradient over one short section of line is as steep as 1 in 46. *Ken Wightman / David Clark collection*

Another double-header near Stoneycombe, this time with 'Manor' Class 4-6-0 No.7809 *Childrey Manor* in double harness with a 'Castle' Class locomotive on a westbound train. Both locomotives appear to be 'blowing off' slightly so they must have been steaming very well on this demanding climb. The milepost on the left of the shot is misleading because it indicates the mileage from London Paddington via Bristol which was the route taken by trains from London to the west of England until the Castle Cary to Taunton line was completed in 1906. *John Ashman F.R.P.S.*

In this portrait taken in the early 1950s, No.7809 *Childrey Manor* and an unidentified 'King' Class locomotive are seen storming up the bank on the down 'Cornish Riviera Express'; the pair were photographed just before they entered the eastern portal of Dainton tunnel. Note that the 'King' is carrying a 'Cornish Riviera Limited' headboard but in the 1954 public timetable the train was advertised as the 'Cornish Riviera Express', suggesting that this shot was taken before 1954. The embankment on the right appears to have been set on fire by flying sparks, judging by the burnt grass. *Childrey Manor*, clearly a favourite for piloting work over the south Devon banks, was based at Laira (Plymouth) in the early 1950s but was transferred to Newton Abbot at some stage, being allocated to that shed in May 1958. It was re-allocated to Cardiff (Canton) later in that year but by late 1961 was based at Oswestry for use on the Cambrian lines. *John Ashman F.R.P.S.*

Unlike the three previous pictures of trains on Dainton bank, this illustration shows an eastbound working. The severity of the climb from Totnes to Dainton summit can be gauged from this illustration of No.4087 *Cardigan Castle* which has just reached the top of the incline and is about to enter the western end of the tunnel. The gradients against eastbound trains vary from a relatively moderate 1 in 65 to a half-mile stretch of 1 in 38. *Cardigan Castle* has just passed Dainton Tunnel signal box and sidings, on the left, with a working from Plymouth. A notice instructing drivers of goods trains to stop to pin down brakes can be seen in front of the signal box. *John Ashman F.R.P.S.*

NEWTON ABBOT TO PLYMOUTH

Situated in a valley formed by the river Dart, Totnes was approached by very steep main-line descents in both directions, with Dainton summit to the east and Rattery to the west, this being in part a legacy of Brunel's misguided atmospheric experiment. In complete contrast, branch trains to/from Ashburton merely ambled along beside the normally placid waters of the river Dart and did not have any ferocious gradients to contend with! In this picture, taken in 1958, Bulleid 'West Country' Class No.34002 *Salisbury* is seen getting into its stride after leaving Totnes with an Exeter to Plymouth local train, probably the 11.35am from Exeter St David's. Appearances of SR motive power on this WR route were normally for route familiarisation purposes (as previously mentioned) and it is likely this train was one of those. The Bulleid 'Pacifics' were noted among footplate crews for their hill climbing abilities, but it is doubtful whether these would be severely tested by the modest four-coach formation seen here. *Colin Hogg*

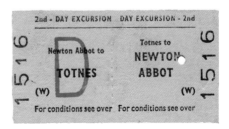

Brent station is the location of this photograph which depicts a rather dirty former GWR 4300 Class 2-6-0 No.6391 pausing with (what appears to be) a local working from Plymouth to Newton Abbot or Exeter. Brent station was opened by the South Devon Railway in about 1849 and lasted until 5th October 1964. It was the junction for the Kingsbridge branch until the closure of that line from 16th September 1963; branch trains departed from the down loop line platform.
Ken Wightman / David Clark collection

The west end of Brent station is seen in this portrait of 'County' Class 4-6-0 No.1014 *County of Glamorgan* pulling away in the evening sunshine on 26th August 1961. It would have been an easy run for the crew from there to Plymouth with the gradients in their favour but, of course, caution would have been needed when descending Hemerdon bank. *R.C. Riley*

Full blast! 'Grange' Class 4-6-0 No. 6865 *Hopton Grange* assists an unidentified 'Castle' up Hemerdon bank with an eastbound express on 2nd April 1956. Hemerdon bank started just beyond Plympton station where the initial gradient was 1 in 41, but this moderated, if that is quite the right word, to 1 in 47 before steepening to 1 in 42 for almost two miles before the summit was reached. One can only imagine the deafening noise being emitted by the two locomotives which were probably working 'flat out' as they passed the photographer. *Colin Hogg*

Another masterpiece on Hemerdon bank. Watched by a young couple with a young child in a pushchair on the adjacent roadway, BR Standard Class 4MT 4-6-0 No.75028 gives 'Castle' Class 4-6-0 No.4090 *Dorchester Castle* a helping hand up the stiff gradient with the 12am Penzance to Manchester/Glasgow on 2nd April 1956. The two locomotives are pulling a massive load of at least 13 coaches and their exhaust noise doubtless shattered the peace of this rural area on the eastern outskirts of Plymouth. What a wonderful spectacle! The scheduled arrival time of this train in Glasgow was 7.20am the following morning and it is interesting to note that it was routed via Shrewsbury and Liverpool (Lime Street). No.75028 was one of a handful of these machines allocated to Plymouth (Laira) at the time but they were later transferred away from the area with the result that engines of this class became extremely rare on the Plymouth to Newton Abbot line. *Colin Hogg*

An aerial view of some of the once substantial railway installations at Laira, about two miles east of Plymouth station, on 17th July 1960. The main line from Plymouth to Newton Abbot is on the left of the picture, while the route to the former 'Southern' Plymouth Friary station, which had been closed to passengers by this date, is on the right. The two lines converged at Laira Junction, the location of which is marked by the signal box located just in front of the roadbridge. The picture appears to have been taken from the top of Laira depot's coaling plant, an excellent vantage point for a panoramic picture. This shed was in a triangle of lines, the other side of the triangle being out of the picture some distance behind the photographer. This was the line from Plymouth Friary (Mount Gould Junction) to Lipson Junction that enabled 'Southern' trains from the Friary station to reach Plymouth North Road, the former GWR station, before branching off towards Devonport (Kings Road), Bere Alston and Tavistock. The stretch of water in the background beyond the roadway is the estuary of the river Plym. *R.C. Riley*

Laira shed, Plymouth, on Sunday 9th July 1961, before steam traction had been ousted. The shed in the middle of the shot is a roundhouse opened in 1901 to relieve the congested premises at Millbay which dated from 1849. The building to the left of the diesel locomotives was constructed in 1931 and consisted of four roads; it was known locally as the 'long shed'. Sandwiched between the two separate sheds is the stores building, while on the extreme left part of the new diesel depot is visible. Laira shed's coaling stage, topped with a 45,000 gallon water tank, is on the right while behind it sits a wartime extension. The main Plymouth to Newton Abbot line is on the extreme right behind the rows of locomotives. *R.C. Riley*

A most interesting picture showing the remains of the 4ft 6in gauge Lee Moor tramway where it crossed the main Plymouth to Newton Abbot line on the level near Laira Junction. The tramway, which had a chequered history, was built by the Tavistock & South Devon Railway between Plymouth and Lee Moor and opened in September 1854, but almost immediately closed following an accident on one of the cable-operated inclines. It was rebuilt and re-opened in September 1858 and then entered a period of relative prosperity with increasing clay traffic from the quarries at Lee Moor. Locomotives were used on the sections between the two inclines while horses were employed elsewhere. The tramway closed in 1939 but partially re-opened after the Second World War; by 1958, however, it was largely overgrown with decaying rolling stock and track. The last train reportedly ran over a short section on 26th August 1960. The track, apart from the crossing visible here, was finally lifted in the 1961/62 period as this picture, which was taken on 27th August 1961, verifies. Note that while the track on the other side of the main line beyond the level crossing gate has been removed, a signal controlling trains on the tramway remains defiantly in position! *R.C. Riley*

Super power on the 'Cornish Riviera Express'. This photograph depicts Plymouth North Road station as it was on 12th July 1955 when steam was still king on the Paddington trains, carmine and cream was the standard livery and old GWR lower quadrant signals controlled movements throughout the station. The unidentified locomotives waiting to leave at the head of the 'Cornish Riviera Express' are a 'Castle' and a 'King', and, judging by its immaculate condition, the latter had obviously been the subject of lavish attention by the cleaners at Laira shed. Note the different types of tenders; the 'Castle' has a Hawksworth flat sided tender while the 'King' is running with one of the more common Collett-type tenders. The first station on this site opened in March 1877 and was enlarged in 1908. Rebuilding work started in 1938 but was halted by the outbreak of hostilities during the following year. In 1956 work re-started and included a ten-storey office block to accommodate the staff of BR's Plymouth division; the new station opened in 1962. When Plymouth Friary station, the 'Southern' terminus in the city, closed on 15th September 1958 the name of the station was abbreviated to simply 'Plymouth'. *R.C. Riley*

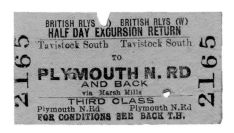

The Churchward 4700 Class 2-8-0s were built shortly after the First World War to work fitted goods trains but they were nothing if not versatile machines and were often seen on passenger work during the peak summer months when the motive power department was hard pressed for locomotives. In this picture No.4700, in respectably clean condition, is seen at the western end of Newton Abbot station powering what is thought to be a Paignton to Plymouth excursion which comprises 'Southern' stock and would have been a most unusual working for one of these locomotives. Newton Abbot station was probably at its busiest on summer Saturdays in the 1950s when holiday traffic was at its height; many trains heading to Paignton changed engines while others attached or detached pilot locomotives for assisting over the south Devon banks. Newton Abbot station was rebuilt in 1927, reportedly at a cost of £140,000. A feature of the new station were

scissors crossovers which connected with through tracks; these apparently speeded-up the movement of trains which were booked to attach or detach portions at the station. The two chimneys prominent above the first coach mark the location of Newton Abbot power station which was supplied with coal trans-shipped at Kingswear and then brought up by rail. This photograph was taken on 4th July 1961.
W. Potter / R.C. Riley collection

Holiday-makers alighting from trains at Torquay would have been given a very favourable first impression of the town by the really stunning display of flowers and shrubs, at the end of the up platform, which looks spectacular despite the overcast conditions. Let us hope the weather improved. Not quite so impressive is the state of the paintwork on the footbridge but never mind! *Stuart Ackley collection*

Contrary to folk lore not all WR express passenger locomotives were kept immaculately clean with polished safety valve bonnets and shining copper capped chimneys. In this illustration 'Castle' Class 4-6-0 No.4078 *Pembroke Castle*, which was allocated to Bristol (Bath Road) shed at the time of this picture, is depicted in absolutely deplorable external condition heading down the Kingswear branch between Torquay and Paignton. The train was photographed passing the gasworks sidings on 14th June 1959. The gasworks' small diesel shunter is partially visible in the left foreground while on the right can be seen (what appears to be) a war-time pill box. The bay on the right looks very appealing but the backdrop of the local gasworks is unlikely to have endeared it to holiday-makers. *W. Potter / R.C. Riley collection*

The first section of the Kingswear branch was authorised by Parliament in 1846 and opened by the South Devon Railway as far as 'Torquay' (later Torre) on 18th December 1848. A further stretch of line was promoted by the nominally independent Dartmouth & Torbay Railway (D&TR) which faced the challenge of extending the route to Paignton, an extension that involved building 20 bridges, a viaduct and a tunnel that was opened out in 1910. The line opened on 2nd August 1859 and from that date a new station was provided at Torquay and the old 'Torquay' station was renamed Torre. Three more miles were brought into use as far as Brixham Road (later Churston) on 14th March 1861. It was then proposed to take the line across the estuary of the river Dart to the fashionable town of Dartmouth but the House of Lords rejected this idea and the company decided to settle on a line to Kingswear with a steam ferry across the river to Dartmouth 'station'. This accounts for the highly unusual situation whereby Dartmouth had a railway station but no trains. Work on the Brixham Road to Kingswear line commenced in 1862 but was bedevilled by heavy engineering works, including the 495 yards-long Greenway tunnel and two lengthy viaducts, and the opening was delayed until 16th August 1864. The D&TR, including its ferry operations, was absorbed by the SDR in 1872. This picture gives a comprehensive view of Kingswear station, the adjoining quay and the river Dart. The locomotive simmering at the platform in this shot taken on 27th June 1961 is 'Hall' Class No.5920 *Wycliffe Hall* while in the background the quay seems to be very busy with coal trans-shipments, probably *en route* to Newton Abbot power station as previously mentioned. The buildings just visible across the river are in Dartmouth.
W. Potter / R.C. Riley collection

One man's railway. When the South Devon Railway's (SDR) line from Newton Abbot to Kingswear opened in 1864 an intermediate station was provided called Brixham Road (later Churston) but the topography of the area meant that it was not possible to serve the fishing port of Brixham. A local businessman, Mr Richard Wolston, was determined that the town should be connected to the national network and he promoted the broad gauge Torbay & Brixham Railway to link the port with Brixham Road station. When the contractor who had been engaged to build the line defaulted Wolston courageously carried on and completed it with his own workforce. The branch opened for traffic on 28th February 1868 using a second-hand locomotive, an 0-4-0WT *Queen* which dated from 1852. Unfortunately, the line had financially exhausted Wolston but his railway continued on an independent basis until the GWR (who had taken over from the SDR) bought it for a bargain price of £12,000 in 1883. In 1892 the route was converted to standard gauge. It is recorded that until 1896 one driver and fireman worked the entire branch service which resulted in an almost unbelievable 15 hour shift. One of the problems with operating the line concerned the availability of water supplies at Brixham which were pumped up from a stream to the engine shed tank. There was often a shortage of this vital commodity at Brixham but the situation eased when a mains water tower was erected at Churston in 1910. The tiny locomotive shed at Brixham closed in 1929 after which time a locomotive and crew were supplied on a daily basis by Newton Abbot shed. Passenger traffic held up well until 1951 when a coal shortage caused the branch service to be curtailed and many passengers deserted the railway for local buses, never to return. Diesel traction in the form of a single unit DMU took over in 1961 but the branch was still considered to be unremunerative and closed from 13th May 1963 – no doubt Richard Wolston would have been turning in his grave. Brixham station, with 1400 Class 0-4-2T No.1452 on an auto train working at the platform, is seen on 16th June 1959.
W. Potter / R.C. Riley collection

Western Region 1961 summer timetable

Heathfield, junction for the 'narrow gauge'. It could be said that the Teign Valley line from Newton Abbot to Exeter via Heathfield had a complicated history because the short Heathfield to Ashton section alone apparently needed a total of nine Acts of Parliament before work started. This stretch of line opened as a standard gauge route from Heathfield on 9th October 1882 and remained very much isolated until the Newton Abbot to Moretonhampstead line was converted from broad to standard gauge in May 1892. In 1883 the Exeter Railway was sanctioned to finish the route from Ashton to Exeter St Thomas, but it was a massive undertaking with two tunnels and numerous cuttings which necessitated the removal of huge amounts of spoil, thus delaying the opening to 1st July 1903. The branch was once a useful alternative to the main Exeter to Newton Abbot line via Dawlish, which was susceptible to bad weather, but its steep 1 in 56 gradients reduced its attractiveness as an alternative emergency route and after nationalisation Plymouth traffic took the Okehampton line if the need arose. The branch's mineral traffic withered away and passenger carryings were poor so it must have come as no surprise when the line lost its passenger service from 9th June 1958, the Exeter to Christow section being closed completely. Goods traffic continued between Heathfield and Christow until the track was damaged by flooding near Ashton in September 1960. When this picture of Heathfield station (looking towards Moretonhampstead) was taken on 5th March 1961 the premises had been closed to passengers for almost exactly two years, yet the station appears to be well-kept and all of the signalling seems to be intact. At that time efforts were being made by local people to take over the Moretonhampstead branch and perhaps BR was keeping everything in place just in case they were successful. Alas! *John Langford*

G. W. R.

Heathfield

It is easy to see why the Teign Valley line was not fertile territory for the railway: there is only one building to be seen in this photograph (on the extreme left) apart from the station. This picture was taken at Chudleigh in August 1955 and clearly the goods yard was still open for business: note the wagons in the yard. At the time of this photograph the train service between Newton Abbot and Exeter consisted of five trains in each direction on weekdays only, supplemented by a short return working in the early morning between Exeter and Trusham; there were additional trains on Saturdays. This view was taken looking southwards towards Heathfield. *Stuart Ackley collection*

The apparently newly-painted level crossing gates at Ashton stand out in this picture, looking towards Exeter, which dates from August 1955. The station facilities there do not seem to be too lavish: there is not even a small canopy to protect passengers from the elements, but perhaps an area with seating was provided inside the building. *Stuart Ackley collection*

Christow station had a relatively complicated layout because, in addition to a passing loop, there was also a quarry with various sidings. Part of the quarry can just be discerned behind the trees on the extreme right of the picture while the raft of wagons at the end of the up platform will be noted. The signal box, also partly concealed by trees, is located at the end of the down platform. An Exeter to Heathfield train, hauled by an unidentified 4575 Class locomotive, is seen taking water at Christow on 24th August 1957. *Gerald Daniels*

Table 88 EXETER, CHRISTOW, and HEATHFIELD—(Third class only)

Miles	Week Days only	a.m	a.m	a.m	a.m (Saturdays only)	p.m	p.m	p.m	p.m (Saturdays only)
—	Exeter (St. David's) dep	6 30	7 0	9 44	1145	1249	4 25	6 5	9 30
1	" (St. Thomas)....	6 34	7 4	9 49	1150	1255	4 29	6 10	9 33
2	Alphington Halt.......	6 38	7 9	9 54	1155	1 0	4 34	6 14	9 38
3¼	Ide Halt..............	6 42	7 14	9 58	12 0	1 5	4 39	6 19	9 43
6	Longdown..............	6 49	7 22	10 6	12 8	1 14	4 47	6 27	9 51
7½	Dunsford Halt.........	6 53	7 26	10 9	1212	1 18	4 52	6 31	9 55
9¼	Christow..............	6 58	7 33	1015	1218	1 28	4 58	6 43	10 0
10¾	Ashton................	7 4	7 38	1019	1223	1 33	5 4	6 48	10 5
12¾	Trusham...............	7 10	7 44	1025	1229	1 40	5 10	6 53	1012
14½	Chudleigh.............	..	7 49	1029	1234	1 45	5 15	6 58	1017
15¾	Chudleigh Knighton Halt	..	7 53	1033	1238	1 48	5 19	7 2	1021
17	Heathfield..........arr	..	7 57	1038	1243	1 55	5 24	7 8	1026
20¾	90 Newton Abbot ..arr	..	8 25	1050	..	2 7	5 46	7 34	1036

Miles	Week Days only	a.m	a.m	a.m	p.m (Saturdays only)	p.m	p.m	p.m
	90 Newton Abbot ..dep	..	7 50	1032	1244	3 5	6 5	8 15
—	Heathfield..........dep	..	8 5	1045	1 3	3 15	6 20	8 30
1¼	Chudleigh Knighton Halt	..	8 10	1050	1 9	3 20	6 24	8 34
2½	Chudleigh.............	..	8 14	1053	1 13	3 24	6 28	8 38
4¼	Trusham...............	7 45	8 19	1058	1 20	3 29	6 33	8 43
6¼	Ashton................	7 50	8 24	11 3	1 24	3 34	6 38	8 48
7¾	Christow..............	8 0	8 30	11 8	1 30	3 39	6§55	8 54
9½	Dunsford Halt.........	8 6	8 35	1114	1 35	3 45	7 0	9 0
11	Longdown..............	8 11	8 40	1118	1 40	3 50	7 5	9 5
13¾	Ide Halt..............	8 17	8 46	1125	1 45	3 56	7 12	9 12
15	Alphington Halt.......	8 21	8 50	1129	1 50	4 0	7 16	9 16
16	Exeter (St. Thomas)....	8 27	8 55	1135	1 55	4 6	7 24	9 22
17	" (St. David's)..arr	8 34	9 3	1140	2 0	4 11	7 30	9 27

Western Region 1953–54 winter timetable

The Newton Abbot to Exeter via Heathfield branch followed the valley of the river Teign from Newton Abbot to a point about two miles north of Christow so the description 'Teign Valley line' is a trifle misleading. The line left the Teign valley near Dunsford Halt and, after travelling in a more or less northerly direction from Newton Abbot, ran eastwards through quite hilly terrain for the rest of the way to Exeter. Dunsford Halt was one of three halts on the line opened by the GWR in June 1928 in order to attract more passenger traffic. One of the stations on the northern section of line above Dunsford was Longdown (14¾ miles from Newton Abbot) and in this illustration the 12.45pm from Exeter St David's to Newton Abbot is seen entering the station behind 8750 Class 0-6-0PT No.3606 on 23rd May 1958. *Gerald Daniels*

The Moretonhampstead & South Devon Railway Company was formed in 1861 at a meeting of promoters at the Globe Hotel in Exeter and their plan to construct a 12½ miles-long line from Newton Abbot to Moretonhampstead received the Royal Assent during the following year. Work on the broad gauge line began in 1863 and progress was rapid, there being no major earthworks on the route, and following a Board of Trade inspection the line opened for passengers on 4th July 1866. In 1872 the branch was absorbed by the South Devon Railway which became part of the GWR four years later. The picturesque line climbed 550ft from the main line junction at Newton Abbot to Moretonhampstead and initially had intermediate stations at Teigngrace, Heathfield, Bovey Tracey and Lustleigh. In 1892 the broad gauge track was replaced as part of the wider conversion of the whole network; it is reputed that the task was undertaken by a team of 60 men and the entire operation completed in only 32 hours. Traffic was sparse at first but in 1906 the GWR started running connecting buses to Chagford and the route's tourist potential was recognised as the south-west of England grew in popularity with holiday-makers. The outbreak of hostilities in 1939 put paid to holiday traffic and after the war no effort was apparently made to revive the branch's fortunes, with the result that in 1957 rumours of closure started to circulate. Unfortunately, the rumours were well-founded and the last ordinary passenger trains ran along the line on 28th February 1959. The track was subsequently lifted north of Heathfield but a stub remains *in situ* south thereof for occasional timber and oil traffic. In this illustration an auto train is depicted at Moretonhampstead on an unknown date; note the particularly tidy and well-kept station.
Stuart Ackley collection

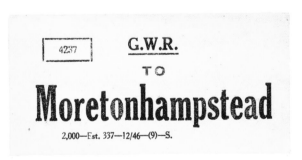

4237

G.W.R.

TO

Moretonhampstead

2,000—Est. 337—12/46—(9)—S.

A further picture of the appealing station at Moretonhampstead taken on 14th July 1959, just over four months after the withdrawal of the passenger service, but it should be noted that goods services still operated at this time and lasted until April 1964. The timber-framed train shed was braced with wrought iron tie rods while the station building, which is partially visible on the left, was constructed of local stone. In the early days an extension to Chagford was contemplated but this scheme never left the drawing board and, perhaps with the extension in mind, the tracks were extended a short way beyond the station building but they merely served the cattle pens. Perhaps the most interesting feature at Moretonhampstead was the engine shed which had the signal box incorporated into a side wall – a most unusual arrangement. Part of the signal box can just be discerned beyond the second telegraph pole in this photograph. The shed was closed in about 1948, a decision that probably resulted in increased 'light engine' movements to and from Newton Abbot. Moretonhampstead station had a lovely remote and peaceful feeling, this being enhanced by its position on the edge of the town which is a gateway to the wilds of Dartmoor. It is to be regretted that such an attractive line has been consigned to history. *R.C. Riley*

Table 90	NEWTON ABBOT, BOVEY, and MORETONHAMPSTEAD—(Third class only)																			
Miles			**Week Days**											**Sundays** (First & Third class)					
		a.m	a.m	a.m	p.m	p.m	p.m		p.m	p.m	p.m			a.m G	a.m G	p.m G	p.m G	
—	Newton Abbot......dep	7 50	9 20	1032	..	1244	2 15	3 5	..	4 30	6 5	8 15	..	..	8 40	..	1140	..	3 55	..	7 48	..	..
2¼	Teigngrace Halt........	7 54	9 24	1035	..	1249	2 19	3 10	..	4 33	6 8	8 19	..	..	8 43	..	1144	..	3 59	..	7 52	..	..
3¼	Heathfield............	8 0	9 29	1042	..	1253	2 23	3 14	..	4 38	6 13	8 23	..	..	8 48	..	1148	..	4 3	..	7 56	..	..
5¼	Brimley Halt..........	8 4	9 33	1047	..	1257	2 27	..	..	4 42	6 17	8 28	..	..	8 52	..	1152	..	4 7	..	8 0	..	..
6	Bovey...............	8 10	9 36	1051	..	1 1	2 30	..	..	4 45	6 20	8 31	..	..	8 55	..	1155	..	4 10	..	8 3	..	..
7¼	Hawkmoor Halt.......	8 15	9 41	1056	..	1 6	2 35	..	..	4 50	6 25	8 36	..	..	9 0	..	12 0	..	4 15	..	8 8	..	..
8¾	Lustleigh............	8 19	9 45	11 0	..	1 10	2 39	..	..	4 55	6 29	8 40	..	..	9 5	..	12 4	..	4 19	..	8 12	..	..
12¼	Moretonhampstead. arr	8 31	9 57	1111	..	1 21	2 51	..	..	5 6	6 42	8 52	..	..	9 16	..	1216	..	4 31	..	8 24	..	..

Miles			**Week Days**											**Sundays** (First & Third class)					
		a.m	a.m	a.m	a.m	p.m	p.m	p.m	p.m	p.m	p.m	S		a.m G	p.m G	p.m G	p.m G	
—	Moretonhampstead dep	7 50	8 40	1015	1135	..	1 35	..	3 15	5 15	..	7 0	..	9 30	..	1 30	..	4 40	..	8 30	..	..
3½	Lustleigh............	7 59	8 48	1023	1144	..	1 43	..	3 23	5 23	..	7 8	..	9 38	..	1 38	..	4 48	..	8 38	..	..
4¾	Hawkmoor Halt.......	8 1	8 50	1025	1146	..	1 45	..	3 25	5 25	..	7 10	..	9 40	..	1 40	..	4 50	..	8 40	..	..
6¼	Bovey...............	8 8	8 54	1030	1151	..	1 50	..	3 30	5 30	..	7 15	..	9 45	..	1 45	..	4 55	..	8 45	..	..
7	Brimley Halt..........	8 11	8 58	1034	1155	..	1 53	..	3 32	5 32	..	7 18	..	9 48	..	1 48	..	4 58	..	8 48	..	..
8½	Heathfield............	8 16	9 3	1040	12 0	..	1 58	2 27	3 39	5 37	..	7 24	1027	9 53	..	1 53	..	5 3	..	8 53	..	..
10¼	Teigngrace Halt........	8 20	9 7	1045	12 4	..	2 2	2 30	3 43	5 40	..	7 28	1030	9 57	..	1 57	..	5 7	..	8 57	..	..
12½	Newton Abbot ...arr	8 25	9 12	1050	1211	..	2 7	2 40	3 50	5 46	..	7 34	1036	10 3	..	2 3	..	5 13	..	9 3	..	..

G Commences 2nd May, 1954.   **S** Saturdays only.
A Road Motor Service is operated by the **Devon General Omnibus Company** between **Moretonhampstead & Chagford.**

Western Region 1953–54 winter timetable; first class accommodation was available on Sundays

Country branch line stations do not come much prettier than Lustleigh, 8¾ miles from Newton Abbot, which is seen here in this photograph that is thought to date from the mid-1950s; this view was taken looking southwards. Lustleigh station served a small settlement that nestled in a valley formed by one of the tributaries of the river Bovey and is likely to have been a quiet rural station, where the station staff's daily routine was only occasionally interrupted by the appearance of a passenger. At least the modest station building was kitted out with an impressive display of BR notices, doubtless extolling the advantages of rail travel, but the meagre service of only eight trains in each direction – on weekdays only – probably did little to encourage prospective passengers. In 1955 the last train back from Newton Abbot was at 8.15pm so even an 'evening out' to the pictures would have been out of the question. Note the tiny goods yard with its couple of wagons – presumably the local coal merchant operated from there – while of more interest is the clerestory coach at the end of the siding. Lustleigh would have been the perfect location for a camping coach and perhaps that is what it was! *Stuart Ackley collection*

There had been several ideas to link the towns of Buckfastleigh and Ashburton to the fast-growing national rail system and in 1848 a scheme to connect Ashburton with Newton Abbot received the Royal Assent and none other than Isambard Kingdom Brunel was asked to be the engineer for the line. The economy was in recession, however, and despite Brunel's involvement the plan was abandoned. Eventually another scheme was promoted and this envisaged a broad gauge line running alongside the river Dart from Buckfastleigh to connect with the South Devon Railway at Totnes. The grandly named Buckfastleigh, Totnes and South Devon Railway was incorporated in 1864 and gained powers during the following year for an extension to Ashburton; the line opened on 1st May 1872. The branch was taken over by the GWR, successor to the SDR, in 1878 and in May 1892 the entire line was converted to standard gauge, this operation apparently being completed during a single weekend. Coal, wool and general agricultural traffic were the lifeblood of the branch for many years but the growth of private car ownership caused a rapid decline in receipts, the passenger trains being withdrawn from 3rd November 1958, well before 'Beeching' became a household name. Goods trains ran until 7th September 1962, and this quiet and very attractive little backwater, which had never made a profit in its life, looked set to fade into oblivion. However a group of businessmen vowed to take over the branch to run steam-operated trains for

tourists and holiday-makers. On 2nd October 1965 the first items of rolling stock arrived at Buckfastleigh and the first passenger trains ran on the newly created Dart Valley Railway on 5th April 1969. Sadly, the section north of Buckfastleigh was commandeered for a road scheme. In early 1991 ownership of the line passed to the volunteers who operated it and today the line is known as the South Devon Railway. The interior of the classic little Brunel station at Ashburton is seen in this picture which dates from the early 1960s, by which time the premises were out of use – a really tragic loss for the preservation movement. *Lens of Sutton Association*

A further view of the delightful station at Ashburton showing 1400 Class 0-4-2T No.1470 waiting to leave with a train to Totnes on 18th July 1957. Part of the goods shed is visible on the left of the shot. What a superb preserved branch line terminus this would have been! *Lens of Sutton Association*

The idyllic setting of Buckfastleigh station is clearly apparent from this picture, taken looking towards Totnes, which dates from the early 1960s. The principal building was located on the right-hand platform and this consisted of the usual booking office and waiting rooms. The goods shed is clearly visible, also on the right, together with a large nameboard which left passengers in no doubt regarding the identity of the station. The goods yard consisted of three sidings, two of which had access to cattle docks. The left-hand platform, such as it was, does not seem to have been used by passenger trains and the instructions to staff stipulated that if passenger and goods trains were crossed here the former must be held at the main platform. It must have been a wonderful occasion when the Dart Valley Railway (as it was then known) was formally opened by Lord Beeching on 21st May 1969, but what a shame the section on to Ashburton had to be sacrificed. *Lens of Sutton Association*

Table 92			TOTNES and ASHBURTON—(Third class only)													
			Week Days only													
Miles		a.m	a.m	a.m	p.m	p.m S	p.m	p.m	p.m							
—	Totnes..........dep	..	8 45	1046	1218	1 40	3 25	4 48	6 45	..	..	..	..	..	..	..
3½	Staverton..........	7 52	8 53	1054	1226	1 48	3 33	4 56	6 53	..	..	..	..	..	..	..
7	Buckfastleigh..........	8 0	9 1	11 2	1234	1 56	3 41	5 4	7 1	..	..	..	..	..	..	..
9½	Ashburton.......arr	8 7	9 7	11 8	1240	2 3	3 47	5 10	7 7	..	..	..	..	..	..	..
			Week Days only													
Miles		a.m	a.m	a.m	a.m	p.m S	p.m	p.m	p.m							
—	Ashburton......dep	7 15	8 12	9 30	1125	1255	2 45	4 5	5 45	..	..	..	..	..	..	..
2½	Buckfastleigh	7 20	8 17	9 35	1131	1 0	2 51	4 11	5 51	..	..	..	..	..	..	..
6½	Staverton.....	7 28	8 25	9 43	1139	1 8	2 59	4 19	5 59	..	..	..	..	..	..	..
9½	Totnes..........arr	7 35	8 32	9 50	1146	1 15	3 6	4 27	6 5	..	..	..	..	..	..	..

S Saturdays only.

Western Region 1953–54 winter timetable

The 12½ miles-long line from Brent, on the main line from Exeter to Plymouth, was a lovely backwater which served the South Hams area of Devon but the local populace apparently valued their isolation and were opposed to the building of a line serving their district. The main line had opened in 1848 and ideas for a branch to Kingsbridge were not approved by Parliament until 1864, but only limited progress was made before the promoters ran out of capital. In July 1882 the grandly named Kingsbridge & Salcombe Railway Co. Ltd. was formed and the branch eventually opened to traffic as far as Kingsbridge on 19th December 1893, a mere 29 years since construction was originally approved, but by this time the local concern had been taken over by the GWR. Despite being part of the local company's title, Salcombe was never served by the line. In later years traffic was steadily eroded by the growth in bus services and private motoring; the line came to life on summer Saturdays, however, when through trains to and from Paddington were provided but this was hardly likely to sustain the branch and the inevitable closure came on 16th September 1963. In this portrait a rather dirty 4575 Class 2-6-2T No.5525 sits in the loop at Brent after arriving from Kingsbridge on 26th August 1961 and it is sad to see that, even on a Saturday in the popular holiday month of August, one coach provided sufficient accommodation for those wishing to travel. *R.C. Riley*

Table 93.		BRENT and KINGSBRIDGE (for Salcombe)									
Miles		**Week Days only**									
		a.m	p.m		p.m	p.m	p.m	p.m			
	Brent........dep	8 20	1224	..	4 15	.. 5 20	.. 6 45	.. 9 20	..	..	
2½	Avonwick........	8 27	1230	..	4 22	.. 5 27	.. 6 52	.. 9 27	..	..	
5½	Gara Bridge.........	8 35	1238	..	.. 4 32	.. 5 35	.. 7 0	.. 9 35	..	..	
9	Loddiswell............	8 43	1246	..	4 41	.. 5 43	.. 7 8	.. 9 43	..	..	
12½	Kingsbridge ....arr	8 55	1255	..	4 52	.. 5 55	.. 7 20	.. 9 54	..	..	
—	Salcombe ¶........arr	9 28	.. 1 28		.. 5 28	.. 6 28	.. 8 18	.. 11 3	..	..	

Miles		**Week Days only**								
		a.m	a.m	a.m	p.m	p.m	p.m	p.m		
				S						
—	Salcombe ¶........dep	6 55	1030	1130	1.30	..	3.30	.. 4 30	.. 7 0	..
—	Kingsbridge........dep	7 30	.. 11 0	.. 1220	.. 2 10	.. 4 15	.. 5 15	.. 7 50	..	..
3½	Loddiswell	7 40	1110	1230	2 20	.. 4 25	.. 5 25	.. 8 0	..	..
7	Gara Bridge	7 47	1117	1240	.. 2 27	.. 4 33	.. 5 33	.. 8 8	..	..
10	Avonwick	7 55	1125	1248	.. 2 35	.. 4 42	.. 5 42	.. 8 15	..	..
12½	Brent........arr	8 4	.. 1135	1256	.. 2 45	.. 4 50	.. 5 51	.. 8 24	..	..

S Saturdays only
¶ By Western National Omnibus (6 miles)

Road Services are also operated from Kingsbridge to Thurlestone and Hope

Western Region 1953–54 winter timetable

KINGSBRIDGE BRANCH

If there was a competition for the title of 'the most beautifully situated branch line station in Devon', Gara Bridge, 5½ miles down the line from Brent, would surely be a strong contender. Surrounded by wooded hills and situated on the bank of the river Avon, it could not have been in a more tranquil spot. The peace of the area was only briefly disturbed by six trains each way on weekdays only – there was no Sunday service. Gara Bridge was the sole crossing point between Brent and Kingsbridge so, at least compared to the other intermediate stations on the branch, it was quite important! There was a small goods yard on the left (note the loading gauge) which consisted of a single through road with a short siding to a loading dock. In later years a camping coach was located here, Gara Bridge surely being one of the most sought-after locations for those seeking a truly quiet and undisturbed spot. The accommodation provided was not exactly up to the standard of Paddington's Great Western Royal Hotel but the views were in a class of their own! This shot, looking towards Kingsbridge, was taken in the late 1950s.
Stuart Ackley collection

A platform end scene at Kingsbridge on 20th August 1958 as former GWR 2-6-2T No.5533 takes water prior to taking out the 4.35pm passenger train to Brent. It is likely that locomotives of this class based at Newton Abbot depot spent a week at a time working on the branch and were housed in the small shed at Kingsbridge which was a sub-shed of Newton Abbot. This shed, which is visible on the right of the picture, is unlikely to have had any maintenance facilities or equipment and a replacement engine would probably have been summoned in the event of a failure.
Edwin Wilmshurst

The Kingsbridge branch twisted and turned as it followed the course of the river Avon for most of the way from Brent so, perhaps, it was to be expected that Kingsbridge station would have been built on a curve. This picture shows the colourful flower beds, signal box and the substantial stone-built goods shed, which was fully kitted-out with the regulation fire buckets, on the right hand side. In times gone by horse-drawn carriages plied between Kingsbridge and Salcombe and did a brisk business in the early days meeting the trains.
Ken Wightman / David Clark collection

BRITISH RLYS. (Western Region) (4237)
TO
Kingsbridge

A view from the platform end at Kingsbridge that was probably taken in the late 1950s. The vast majority of branch line terminal stations had a goods yard and many had a small engine shed where a locomotive could be stabled overnight but, most unusually, Kingsbridge also boasted a carriage shed, this being the tunnel-shaped building in the middle of the photograph. This building was made of corrugated iron, painted black and could hold two coaches. The shed was not shown on early official plans so it can be assumed that it was a later addition. In the winter 1954/55 timetable a total of seven trains was advertised in each direction between Brent and Kingsbridge and, with one exception, they stopped at all stations. The exception was the 6.05pm from Kingsbridge which was advertised to run non-stop in 31 minutes, the usual journey time being around 35 minutes. Steam traction reigned unchallenged on the line until 10th June 1961, when the final regular steam-hauled passenger train operated, diesel units taking over for the last two years or so of the branch's life. *Stuart Ackley collection*

The first stretch of the Plymouth to Launceston line was broad gauge and opened by the South Devon & Tavistock Railway which commenced operations to Tavistock on 22nd June 1859. The people of Launceston, just over the Devon county border in Cornwall, desired a rail connection and, after several plans had come to nothing, the Launceston & South Devon Railway obtained an Act of Parliament on 30th May 1862 for a broad gauge line from Launceston across to Lydford and then down to Tavistock to meet the existing route from Plymouth. The opening date for the 19 miles-long line was 1st July 1865. The entire line from Lydford to the junction with the main Newton Abbot to Plymouth route at Tavistock Junction became mixed gauge from 17th May 1876 and was finally converted to standard gauge only in May 1892, by which time the GWR had taken over from the smaller companies. This picture, taken on 29th August 1961, shows Marsh Mills station which was the first one on the branch. The light engine simmering in the foreground is 8750 Class 0-6-0PT No.4673 but probably of greater interest are the two long lines of wagons for the china clay traffic that originated at the works on the horizon. Passenger services were withdrawn from this route at the end of December 1962. *R.C. Riley*

Western Region 1953–54 winter timetable, including the Princetown branch

North of Marsh Mills the line twisted and turned its way through the thickly wooded slopes of the Plym valley, passing Plym Bridge Platform and Bickleigh stations before reaching the tiny and delightfully situated Shaugh Bridge Platform which opened on 21st August 1907. This was equipped with a typical GWR 'pagoda' style waiting shelter, a couple of platform seats and oil lamps which provided the only source of illumination for waiting passengers. This photograph, looking towards Yelverton, was taken on 15th July 1961. *R.C. Riley*

Miles		Week Days																		Suns.		
		a.m	a.m	a.m	a.m	a.m		p.m K	p.m	p.m S	p.m S	p.m	p.m	p.m	p.m	p.m	p.m U	p.m S		p.m C	p.m C	p.m C
—	Launceston .... dep	..	7 10	..	..	10 15	..	..	..	1250	..	2 10	..	..	5 40	..	..	8 25	..	..	..	..
4¾	Lifton	..	7 18	..	..	10 23	..	..	..	1258	..	2 18	..	..	5 48	..	..	8 33	..	..	..	..
8	Coryton	..	7 25	..	..	10 30	..	..	..	1 4	..	2 25	..	..	5 55	..	..	8 39	..	..	..	..
9½	Liddaton Halt	..	7 30	..	..	10 36	..	..	..	1 10	..	2 32	..	..	6 2	..	..	8 44	..	..	..	..
12½	Lydford	..	7 42	..	..	10 46	..	..	..	1N23	..	2 46	..	..	6 17	..	..	8 55	..	..	..	..
15½	Mary Tavy & Blackdown Halt	..	7 49	..	..	10 52	..	..	..	1 28	..	2 51	..	..	6 23	..	..	9 0	..	..	..	..
19	Tavistock South A	6 47	8 U0	8 47	..	11 U2	..	..	1233	1U38	..	3U 4	4 30	..	6U35	7 10	9 15	9H15	..	12 5	4 35	7 15
20	Whitchurch Down Platform.	6 50	8 3	8 50	..	11 5	..	..	1236	1 41	..	3 7	4 33	..	6 39	7 13	9 18	9 18	..	12 8	4 38	7 18
23	Horrabridge	6 57	8 10	8 57	..	11 12	..	..	1243	1 48	..	3 15	4 40	..	6 47	7 20	9 25	9 25	..	1215	4 45	7 25
24½	Yelverton .... arr	7 1	8 15	9 1	..	11 16	..	..	1248	1 52	..	3 19	4 45	..	6 52	7 25	9 29	9 29	..	1220	4 50	7 30
—	Mls Princetown .... dep	..	7 35	..	1030	..	..	12 8	..	..	2 12	..	4 0	6 10	..	..	..	..	..	..	..	..
—	1½ King Tor Halt	..	7 40	..	1035	..	..	1213	..	..	2 17	..	4 5	6 15	..	..	..	..	..	..	..	..
—	4¼ Ingra Tor Halt	..	7 49	..	1044	..	..	1222	..	..	2 26	..	4 14	6 24	..	..	..	..	..	..	..	..
—	7¼ Burrator Halt	..	8 0	..	1055	..	..	1232	..	..	2 36	..	4 25	6 35	..	..	..	..	..	..	..	..
—	9 Dousland	..	8 5	..	11 0	..	..	1238	..	..	2 41	..	4 32	6 40	..	..	..	—	..	..	..	..
—	10½ Yelverton .... arr	..	8 10	..	11 7	..	..	1243	..	..	2 47	..	4 38	6 45	..	..	..	..	..	..	..	..
—	Yelverton .... dep	7 2	8 16	9 2	..	11 18	..	..	1249	1 53	..	3 20	4 46	..	6 57	7 26	9 30	9 30	..	1221	4 51	7 31
25½	Clearbrook Halt	7 5	8 19	9 5	..	11 21	..	..	1253	1 56	..	3 23	4 49	..	7 0	7 29	9 32	9 32	..	1224	4 54	7 34
26¾	Shaugh Bridge Platform	7 8	8 22	9 8	..	11 24	..	..	1256	1 59	..	3 26	4 52	..	7 3	7 32	9 35	9 35	..	1227	4 57	7 37
27¾	Bickleigh	7 11	8 26	9 11	..	11 28	..	..	1 0	2 3	..	3 29	4 57	..	7 6	7 35	9 38	9 38	..	1230	5 0	7 40
30½	Plym Bridge Platform	7 16	8 31	..	..	11 33	..	..	1 5	2 8	..	—	5 2	..	7 11	..	..	..	..	1235	5 5	7 45
31¾	Marsh Mills	7 20	8 35	9 19	..	11 38	..	..	1 10	2 12	..	3 36	5 8	..	7 16	7 42	9 46	9 46	..	1239	5 9	7 49
34¾	Plymouth (N'th Road) ... arr	7 33	8 47	9 26	..	11 47	..	..	1 20	2 20	..	3 50	5 15	..	7 25	7 50	10 0	10 0	..	1247	5 17	8 0

A 1 mile to Tavistock North Station
B Arr. 1 1 p.m.
C Commences 11th April, 1954
E Except Saturdays
g Arr. 11 28 a.m.
H Arr. 9 7 p.m.
K Tues., Thurs, and Sats.
L Arr. 7 55 a.m.
N Arr. 1 20 p.m.
S Saturdays only
U Except Saturdays. Commences 3rd May, 1954
U Arr. 4 minutes *earlier*

Timetable continued from previous page

Horrabridge was another pretty little station on the Launceston line and in this illustration a 4575 Class 2-6-2T, No.5541, is depicted passing through in charge of a southbound goods train on 7th July 1961. The booking office and waiting room were located on the 'up' side platform, together with the signal box, while the 'down' platform was equipped with only a simple waiting shelter. There was also a small goods yard complete with a shed and crane. Horrabridge was privileged to enjoy a period as a junction station because trains to Princetown started and terminated there between August 1883 and May 1885 prior to the opening of Yelverton station. *R.C. Riley*

The train depicted in the previous photograph is seen again, this time passing Mary Tavy & Blackdown Halt which was further up the line beyond Tavistock. The photographer was presumably chasing the train by car and took advantage of the train's stop at Tavistock to undertake a little shunting – note that the consist is different. By the date of this picture Mary Tavy & Blackdown station, which was officially referred to as a 'halt' in the public timetable, had been unstaffed for over 20 years but at least it still had a platform seat and lamp for the convenience of any remaining passengers. The signal box stands as a reminder of much busier times between 1876 and 1890 when this line was mixed gauge and LSWR trains shared the single track with the GWR. In 1890 the LSWR gained its own independent route into Plymouth via Bere Alston over the tracks of the independent Plymouth, Devonport & South Western Junction Railway. The SR Okehampton to Plymouth main line runs in a cutting behind the train.
R.C. Riley

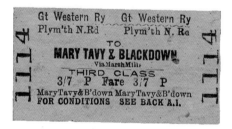

A closer view of Mary Tavy & Blackdown station and its rather battered nameboard. The adjacent signal box seems to be in remarkably good condition after many years of disuse. In times past there was a passing loop here but it was taken out of use in 1892, two years after LSWR trains stopped using the line. The principal settlement served by the station was the village of Mary Tavy which was under a mile from the station, but it was situated on the main Okehampton to Tavistock road and local buses were probably more convenient for the villagers.
R.C. Riley

The LSWR's Plymouth to Exeter via Okehampton main line and the GWR's Plymouth to Launceston branch ran almost parallel to one another between Tavistock and Lydford, where the latter turned off in a westerly direction. Lydford station was served by both routes and was, in effect, two stations side by side. Northbound trains on the former LSWR route and southbound workings on the former GWR line stopped at the middle platform. Perhaps, if the companies had swallowed their pride and co-operated with each other, traffic could have been concentrated on one route between Plymouth and Lydford which may have survived the Beeching cuts and offered a viable alternative to the exposed coastal line between Plymouth and Exeter which is so prone to flooding. This June 1962 picture shows the former GWR platforms at Lydford with a Launceston train approaching. *R. C. Riley*

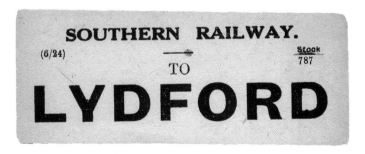

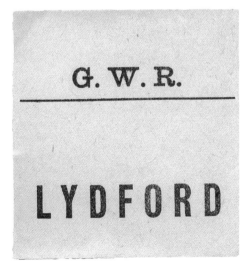

After leaving Lydford the Launceston branch traversed Lydford forest before reaching Coryton, a station almost literally in the middle of nowhere, which is seen here looking towards Tavistock. The tiny village was about a mile away and consisted of little more than a church and a few cottages. The traffic potential of the Launceston line can be gauged by the sparse train service that was on offer in the winter 1954/55 timetable, well before the advent of mass private motoring. There were only four trains throughout on Mondays to Fridays, with two extra workings on Saturdays; additional services ran between Plymouth and Tavistock and this section also had a Sunday service in the summer months. Journey time for the 34¾ miles-long trip between Plymouth and Launceston was on average just over 1½ hours. Needless to say the road between the two places was much more direct! *R.C. Riley*

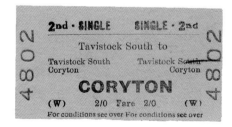

PLYMOUTH TO LAUNCESTON

The branch line to the desolate moors. The beginnings of the Princetown branch can be traced way back to 1823 when the 4ft 6in gauge Plymouth & Dartmoor tramway opened principally to convey granite from King Tor, near Princetown, but lime, sea sand, coal and timber were also carried on the 23 miles-long line. Due to the nature of the terrain the line followed an extremely circuitous route, the distance between Sutton Pool, Plymouth, and King Tor being only 13 miles as the crow flies. The tramway soon fell upon hard times, however, and on 11th August 1883 the GWR opened a standard gauge branch from Yelverton, on the Plymouth to Tavistock line, to Princetown using much of the course of the old tramway which the GWR had bought for £22,000. It should be noted that initially trains ran to and from Horrabridge, because Yelverton

station did not open until 1st May 1885. Dartmoor prison is located at Princetown and in the early years convicts, prison officers and their supplies were a regular source of income though, presumably, the convicts did not pay any fare! Granite from King Tor also helped to sustain the railway, but as time went on, excursionists became the most numerous passengers, though not sufficiently so to prevent closure which occurred from 5th March 1956 with the last trains running on 3rd March. So, this remote, windswept and incomparable by-way, where incredible 1 in 40 gradients took passengers up into the clouds at a height of 1,373ft above sea level, was no more but much of the line's course can still be traced today. This picture, which dates from 5th July 1955, shows a train to Princetown waiting to depart from Yelverton station with 4400 Class 2-6-2T No.4410 in charge. Strangely, the junction with the Princetown line faced Tavistock so through running from Princetown to Plymouth, which was surely more desirable, was not possible without a time-consuming reversal. Note the inspection pit and 23ft 6in turntable. *R.C. Riley*

When the Princetown branch was originally opened there was only one intermediate station, Dousland, and in this photograph the signalman is seen on the platform holding the single line staff, doubtless before retreating into his cosy cabin. Another gentleman strolls up the platform ramp – perhaps he was a prospective passenger. In contrast to the other intermediate stations on the line – which were merely halts – the station here at least seems to have a reasonable building. The train seen here was heading to Princetown and this shot was also taken on 5th July 1955. *R.C. Riley*

After Dousland the next station down the line (from Yelverton) was Burrator and Sheepstor Halt, opened on 4th February 1924, and in this view a mixed train consisting of a passenger coach, two vans and a brake van is seen pulling away towards Princetown from the rather basic platform that comprised the halt's meagre facilities. Perhaps the shed on the extreme right of the picture was a waiting shelter – a welcome refuge for passengers when the unpredictable Dartmoor weather took a turn for the worse. The scenery at this point was particularly spectacular with Burrator reservoir and the wooded slopes beyond forming the backdrop. This picture was also taken on 5th July 1955. *R.C. Riley*

Three halts with rudimentary facilities, Burrator, Ingra Tor and King Tor, were built between the wars, and this shot of the extremely exposed halt at Ingra Tor was also taken on 5th July 1955. A mixed train from Princetown can be seen coming down the gradient. Presumably the halt was built solely for walkers because there is no habitation in the shot at all, and not even a road to 'civilisation'. Like the halt seen in the previous picture, a small hut served as a waiting shelter for passengers and, no doubt, livestock when weather conditions worsened. This halt, which was opened on 2nd March 1936, was famous for an official notice warning people about the presence of snakes. *R.C. Riley*

PRINCETOWN BRANCH

The Turnchapel branch was opened by the LSWR on 1st January 1897 and ran from a junction with the Yealmpton line at Plymstock; its tracks continued beyond Turnchapel station for a further ½ mile to wharfs on the river Plym. Services along the Turnchapel branch started from Plymouth Friary station, the journey time for the 2½ miles-long trip being about ten minutes. In October 1905 Lucas Terrace Halt, situated just to the east of Plymouth Friary engine shed, was opened and this was also served by Turnchapel trains. Some staff at the depot may have found the halt particularly convenient! Services along the Turnchapel branch were suspended between January and July 1951 due to a fuel crisis and, not surprisingly, very few passengers returned to the railway. The branch closed to passengers permanently from 10th September 1951 but goods trains continued for a further ten years, ceasing from 2nd October 1961. In this portrait O2 Class 0-4-4T No.30182 is seen at Oreston with the 12.48pm Plymouth Friary to Turnchapel train on 19th June 1950. *J.J. Smith collection / Bluebell Railway Museum*

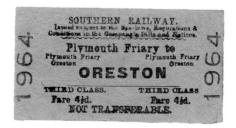

Incredibly, the terminus at Turnchapel was situated in an old quarry and possessed the minimum of facilities, merely a basic waiting shelter on the sole platform. In this shot a Plymouth Friary-bound train is seen at Turnchapel on 19th June 1950. The station depicted here was approached across a swingbridge over a creek and, in addition, there was a short tunnel beyond the station which led to the wharfs, so it used to be quite a fascinating spot. The train was formed of a two-coach pull-push set, which was one of three ordered by the LSWR in 1913 for use on various branch lines in the west country. Originally lit by gas they were converted to electricity in 1919/20. These sets had fabricated metal gates, which gave them a very distinctive appearance, and they were universally known as 'gate sets'. *J.J. Smith collection / Bluebell Railway Museum*

4868

SOUTHERN RAILWAY
This Ticket is issued subject to the Company's Bye-laws, Regulations and Conditions in their Time Tables, Notices and Book of Regulations.

Available only for one journey in either direction.
To be shown on demand.

THIRD CLASS SINGLE
Fare 3½d
BETWEEN

Plymouth Friary
AND
Turnchapel

This Ticket must be punched in the section in which the Passenger is entitled to travel.
A6315

TURNCHAPEL BRANCH